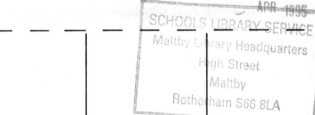

EXPLORERS

EXPEDITIONS AND PIONEERS

Series Editor:
David Salariya was born in Dundee, Scotland, where he studied illustration and printmaking, concentrating on book design in his post graduate year. He later completed a further post-graduate course in art education at Sussex University. He has illustrated a wide range of books on botanical, historical and mythical subjects. He has designed and created many new series of children's books for publishers in the UK and overseas. In 1989, he established his own publishing company, The Salariya Book Company Ltd. He lives in Brighton with his wife, the illustrator Shirley Willis.

Author:
Fiona Macdonald studied history at Cambridge University and at the University of East Anglia, where she is a part-time Tutor in Medieval History. She has also taught in schools and adult education, and is the author of numerous books for children on historical topics.

Consultant:
Pieter Van Der Merwe is General Editor of publications at the National Maritime Museum, Greenwich, which he joined as a research historian in 1974. Since then he has been involved in the development of many NMM displays and exhibitions, including aspects of maritime discovery.

Series Editor	**David Salariya**
Book Editor	**Penny Clarke**
Consultant	**Pieter Van Der Merwe**
Artists	**Mark Bergin**
	Gerald Wood
	Mark Peppé
	Dave Antram

First published in 1994
by Watts

Watts
96 Leonard Street
London EC2A 4RH

© The Salariya Book Co Ltd MCMXCIV

ISBN 0-7496-1537-0

Printed in Belgium

A CIP catalogue record for this book is available from the British Library.

Artists
Mark Bergin, pp 6–7, pp 20–21, pp 34–35, pp 36–37, pp 42·43; **Mark Peppé,** pp 8–9, pp 10–11, pp 14–15, pp 16–17, pp 18–19, pp 22–23, pp 28–29, pp 30–31, pp 38–39; **Gerald Wood,** pp 12–13, pp 24–25, pp 26–27, pp 32–33; **Dave Antram,** pp 40–41.

TIMELINES
EXPLORERS

    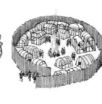 

EXPEDITIONS AND PIONEERS

Written by
FIONA MACDONALD

Created & Designed by
DAVID SALARIYA

WATTS BOOKS
London • New York • Sydney

CONTENTS

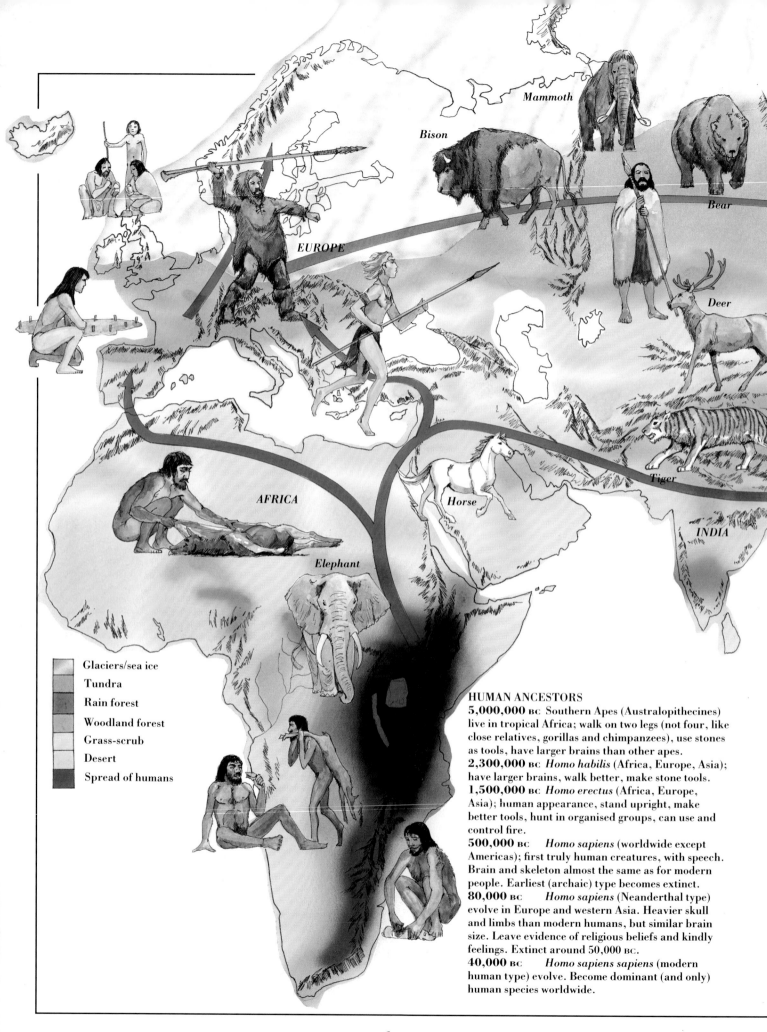

EUROPE

Mammoth

Bison

Bear

Deer

Tiger

Horse

AFRICA

INDIA

Elephant

Glaciers/sea ice
Tundra
Rain forest
Woodland forest
Grass-scrub
Desert
Spread of humans

HUMAN ANCESTORS

5,000,000 BC Southern Apes (Australopithecines) live in tropical Africa; walk on two legs (not four, like close relatives, gorillas and chimpanzees), use stones as tools, have larger brains than other apes.

2,300,000 BC *Homo habilis* (Africa, Europe, Asia); have larger brains, walk better, make stone tools.

1,500,000 BC *Homo erectus* (Africa, Europe, Asia); human appearance, stand upright, make better tools, hunt in organised groups, can use and control fire.

500,000 BC *Homo sapiens* (worldwide except Americas); first truly human creatures, with speech. Brain and skeleton almost the same as for modern people. Earliest (archaic) type becomes extinct.

80,000 BC *Homo sapiens* (Neanderthal type) evolve in Europe and western Asia. Heavier skull and limbs than modern humans, but similar brain size. Leave evidence of religious beliefs and kindly feelings. Extinct around 50,000 BC.

40,000 BC *Homo sapiens sapiens* (modern human type) evolve. Become dominant (and only) human species worldwide.

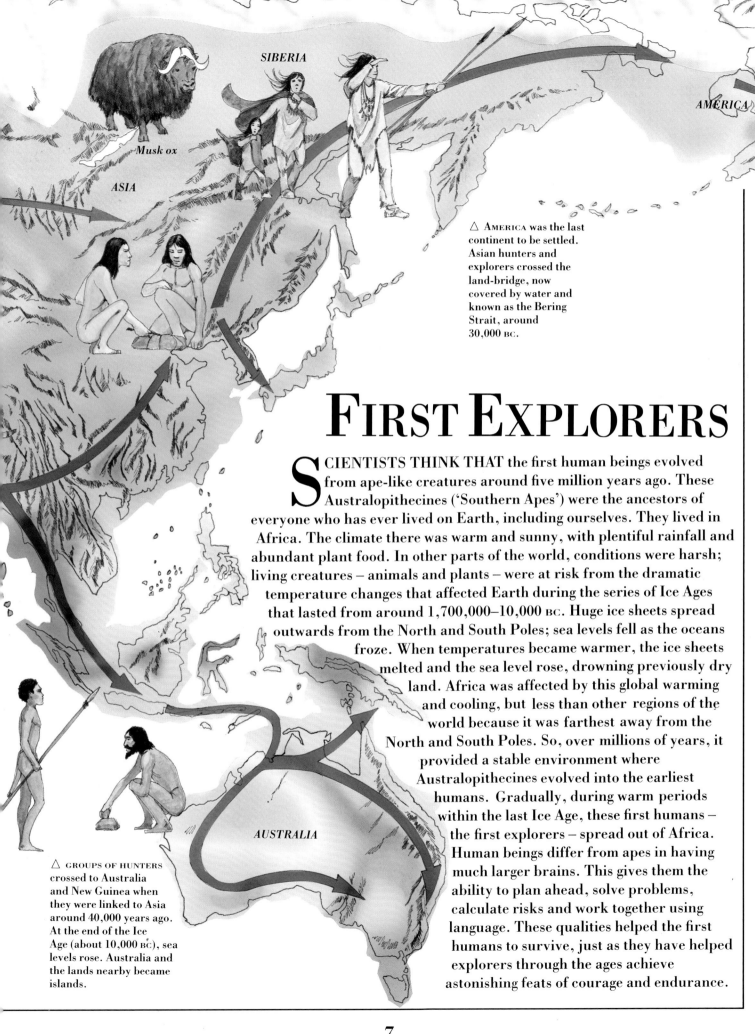

SIBERIA

ASIA

Musk ox

AMERICA

△ AMERICA was the last
continent to be settled.
Asian hunters and
explorers crossed the
land-bridge, now
covered by water and
known as the Bering
Strait, around
30,000 BC.

FIRST EXPLORERS

SCIENTISTS THINK THAT the first human beings evolved
from ape-like creatures around five million years ago. These
Australopithecines ('Southern Apes') were the ancestors of
everyone who has ever lived on Earth, including ourselves. They lived in
Africa. The climate there was warm and sunny, with plentiful rainfall and
abundant plant food. In other parts of the world, conditions were harsh;
living creatures – animals and plants – were at risk from the dramatic
temperature changes that affected Earth during the series of Ice Ages
that lasted from around 1,700,000–10,000 BC. Huge ice sheets spread
outwards from the North and South Poles; sea levels fell as the oceans
froze. When temperatures became warmer, the ice sheets
melted and the sea level rose, drowning previously dry
land. Africa was affected by this global warming
and cooling, but less than other regions of the
world because it was farthest away from the
North and South Poles. So, over millions of years, it
provided a stable environment where
Australopithecines evolved into the earliest
humans. Gradually, during warm periods
within the last Ice Age, these first humans –
the first explorers – spread out of Africa.
Human beings differ from apes in having
much larger brains. This gives them the
ability to plan ahead, solve problems,
calculate risks and work together using
language. These qualities helped the first
humans to survive, just as they have helped
explorers through the ages achieve
astonishing feats of courage and endurance.

AUSTRALIA

△ GROUPS OF HUNTERS
crossed to Australia
and New Guinea when
they were linked to Asia
around 40,000 years ago.
At the end of the Ice
Age (about 10,000 BC), sea
levels rose. Australia and
the lands nearby became
islands.

7

△ ENGRAVED SEAL, 2300 BC, shows Akkadian merchants bringing treasures to their king.

◁ SUMERIAN TRAVELLERS, around 3000 BC, explored the Tigris and Euphrates rivers in boats made of bundles of reeds.

▽ EGYPTIAN WALL-PAINTING, c.1900 BC, of nomadic Jewish metalworkers who travelled in the desert lands of Sinai and Canaan (in present-day Egypt and Israel).

◁ EGYPTIAN SEA-GOING SHIP, about 25 metres long, built of wood and powered by the wind, caught in a vast single sail, or by men rowing with oars.

△ QUEEN HATSHEPSUT of Egypt, 1504–1481 BC, seen here with the god Amun-Re protecting her, sent five ships to Punt in 1493 BC.

EGYPT

THE MIGHTY KINGDOM OF EGYPT depended on the river Nile. The Nile was its life-blood, bringing water to crops in the fields. The river was also the best way to travel – the land of Egypt was dry and stony, or, in the delta where the Nile flowed into the sea, a boggy swamp. So the Egyptians became skilful sailors, and the Nile was thronged with shipping – cargo boats, fishing rafts, pleasure craft and, at festivals, the great royal barge, which carried the pharaoh in solemn procession along the waterway that nourished his lands.

Egyptian sailors were also adventurous travellers by sea. They made regular journeys along the North African coast, to the prosperous island of Crete, and along the eastern shores of the Mediterranean. There, they encountered the peoples of Akkadia, Babylon and Sumeria – rival empires from Mesopotamia – as well as the Phoenicians (who lived in modern Lebanon) and the many different peoples inhabiting present-day Israel, Syria and Jordan.

◁ ASSYRIAN BARGES, 1000 BC, carried fish and grain up-river. Fishermen travelled on simpler craft – inflated goatskins.

▷ THE VOYAGE to Punt. The earliest known long-distance voyage was made by Pharaoh Snefru in 2600 BC.

Egypt

ARABIA

Red Sea

River Nile

AFRICA

Somalia

△ THE EXPEDITION to Punt carried soldiers, royal officials, and provisions.

△ DOMED MUD-BRICK HOUSE in Punt, with an upper room reached by a ladder.

△ THE PRECIOUS MYRRH trees were carefully packed and carried on board by slaves.

△ BAGS OF GOLD and live baboons were brought from Punt to Queen Hatshepsut.

△ THE ROYAL EXPEDITION completed, the Egyptians set sail for home.

▽ ABOUT 30 men were needed to row Egyptian ships like these. The double mast could be lowered and put away when there was no wind.

Sometimes they fought – many pharaohs were keen to expand the Egyptian empire – but more often they traded, buying balm and spices (used for perfumes and when making mummies), or metals to give sharp edges to their tools and weapons. We know little about these early expeditions. The first sea voyage mentioned in Egyptian records was made in 2600 BC. Sailors travelled to Byblos in Phoenicia to buy timber for building. In 1493 BC, Egyptian explorers carried their ships over the desert to the Red then set sail south. They went to buy gold and incense from the land of Punt, probably present-day Somalia, but no-one is sure.

In the seventh century BC, Phoenician sailors hired by Pharaoh Necho II claimed to have sailed right round Africa. Possibly they were telling the truth.

◁ EGYPTIAN TOMB-PAINTING showing heaps of incense, made from myrrh and other plant gums, used in religious ceremonies and for embalming dead bodies to make mummies.

Phoenician glass beads

THE MEDITERRANEAN

THE COUNTRIES BORDERING the Mediterranean Sea have been called 'the cradle of civilisation'. In North Africa, Greece, Asia Minor and the Levant, many rich and powerful nations flourished between 4,000–400 BC. Strong rulers built splendid palaces and made stern laws. Priests and priestesses worshipped in temples decorated with fine works of art. Scholars studied the stars, made mathematical discoveries and invented writing. Just as important, adventurous navigators sailed their ships along a network of routes criss-crossing the Mediterranean. Their main aim was trade, but their travels helped spread new ideas and inventions, as well.

△ PHOENICIAN SILVER plate, around 700 BC, decorated with Egyptian-style designs.

△ PRECIOUS (but very smelly) Tyrian purple dye was one of the luxury goods traded by Phoenician merchants. It was made using secretions produced by a shellfish, *Murex brandaris*, from the eastern Mediterranean.

◁ PHOENICIAN 'ROUND SHIPS' held huge loads of cargo. They were powered by double ranks of rowers and steered by twin stern oars.

▽ LANDS EXPLORED BY Alexander the Great of Macedon and his army of 35,000 men between 334–323 BC. Alexander died in 323 BC but the influence of the Greek civilisation he introduced to Asia lasted for hundreds of years.

△ THE GREEK scholar Herodotus (5th century BC) compiled a book about the Greeks' knowledge of the world.

1 334 BC Alexander leaves Greece; sets out to conquer Asia.
2 Defeats strong Persian army at Granicus river.
3 332 BC Marches south; captures rich ports of Tyre and Sidon.
4 Goes to Egypt; founds city of Alexandria.

Black Sea

EUROPE

ASIA MINOR

Macedon

Greece

Mediterranean Sea

Tyre

Sidon

Egypt

Alexandria

AFRICA

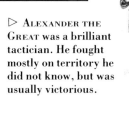

▷ ALEXANDER THE GREAT was a brilliant tactician. He fought mostly on territory he did not know, but was usually victorious.

According to ancient writers, Phoenicians may have ventured as far as Cornwall, to buy tin. Early Greek myths tell how adventurers set out to find gold on the shores of the Black Sea. Later Greek historians recorded the journeys of a fifth-century explorer named Hanno, who told fantastic stories of 'hairy women' (probably chimpanzees) sighted on a trading voyage along the west coast of Africa.

The most famous Greek explorer, Alexander the Great of Macedon (356–323 BC), was not interested in trade. He wanted power. Born a prince in a small but ambitious Greek state, he died aged 32 as ruler of the largest empire in the western world. He achieved this through eleven years of travel, leading an army of largely untrained men across unexplored, inhospitable, mountainous terrain. He conquered remote lands and founded seventy cities. To record his exploits and discoveries, he took with him historians, scientists, engineers and 'steppers' (men who measured distance by counting their steps). At the end of his life, he controlled all the lands between Greece and India – and demanded to be worshipped as a god.

5 New war with Persians; goes back to Mesopotamia; defeats Persian king Darius.
6 Heads eastwards across wild country, chasing Darius.
7 330 BC Darius dies; Alexander marches north; crosses the Khyber Pass, almost 4000 m above sea level.
8 328–7 BC Captures remote kingdom of Bactria; leads army through mountains towards India.
9 326 BC Crosses Indus river. Wants to explore India; army mutinies.
10 Travels west along Indus; proves it is not connected to the Nile.
11 Divides his army; some men to sail home, others to travel by land.
12 Marches by night (when cooler) 200 miles through hot, barren desert; many men die.
13 Fleet short of food and water; mutiny feared. Overland marchers meet fleet at Hormuz; all head inland.
14 323 BC Alexander dies aged 32, at Babylon.

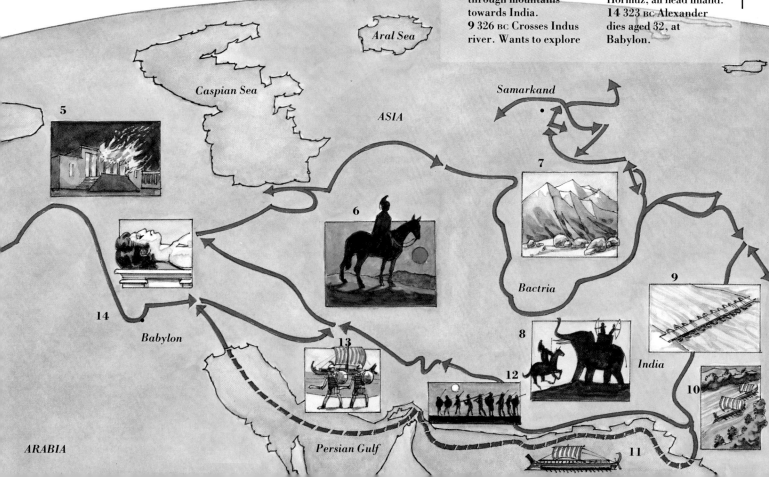

Aral Sea

Caspian Sea

ASIA

Samarkand

5

7

6

Bactria

9

8

India

14

Babylon

13

12

10

ARABIA

Persian Gulf

11

THE ROMAN EMPIRE

THE CITY OF ROME, in Italy, originated around 900 BC as a cluster of mud and timber huts. But by AD 100 Rome ruled the world – or at least almost all the territory known to people living in Europe and the Middle East. How had this happened? Through conquest and trade.

The Roman army was a strong, well-trained and successful fighting machine, and Roman soldiers were seasoned travellers. A campaign to conquer new land usually began with troops being sent to the frontier. This might be hundreds of miles away from Rome – in Germany, Britain or Africa. Armies marched along well-made roads, built after earlier conquests, and camped in tents or in forts constructed quickly of timber. Then scouts surveyed the frontier and spied on enemy forces, while commanders planned the attack. Once new territory was captured, army engineers built more roads, forts and bridges, so the newly-conquered land could easily be controlled from Rome. Men from many different countries joined the Roman army; the pay was good and the foreign travel was exciting. But conditions could be harsh: soldiers from warm Mediterranean lands wrote home for woolly socks as they shivered in icy winds while guarding the Scottish frontier at Hadrian's Wall.

△ A ROMAN ARMY on the move, carved on Marcus Aurelius's Column (c. AD 180) in Rome. Men carry their own food and weapons; extra baggage is loaded on mules.

▷ ROMAN ROADS were built to allow the army to march swiftly throughout the Empire. They were used by travellers and traders too.

▷ THE SEAPORT of Caesarea, in present-day Israel, built by Jewish King Herod the Great, an ally of Rome, in the 1st century BC. Roman engineers helped construct a massive sea wall, over 800 metres long, to provide safe anchorage for merchant ships.

▷ ROMAN MERCHANTS hired heavy, sturdy cargo ships like this to transport valuable cargoes of wine, olive oil and grain. The largest ships could carry over 1,300 tonnes.

ROMAN TOURIST ATTRACTIONS

△ ROMAN NAVY WARSHIPS patrolled busy coastal waters to protect travellers and traders throughout the Roman Empire from pirate attacks. They were fast and easy to manoeuvre, even in calm weather, because they were powered by men rowing as well as by sail.

△ THE ACROPOLIS at Athens, Greece, housed many famous temples, like the Parthenon.

△ SICK PEOPLE prayed to Asclepius, god of healing, at Epidaurus, Greece.

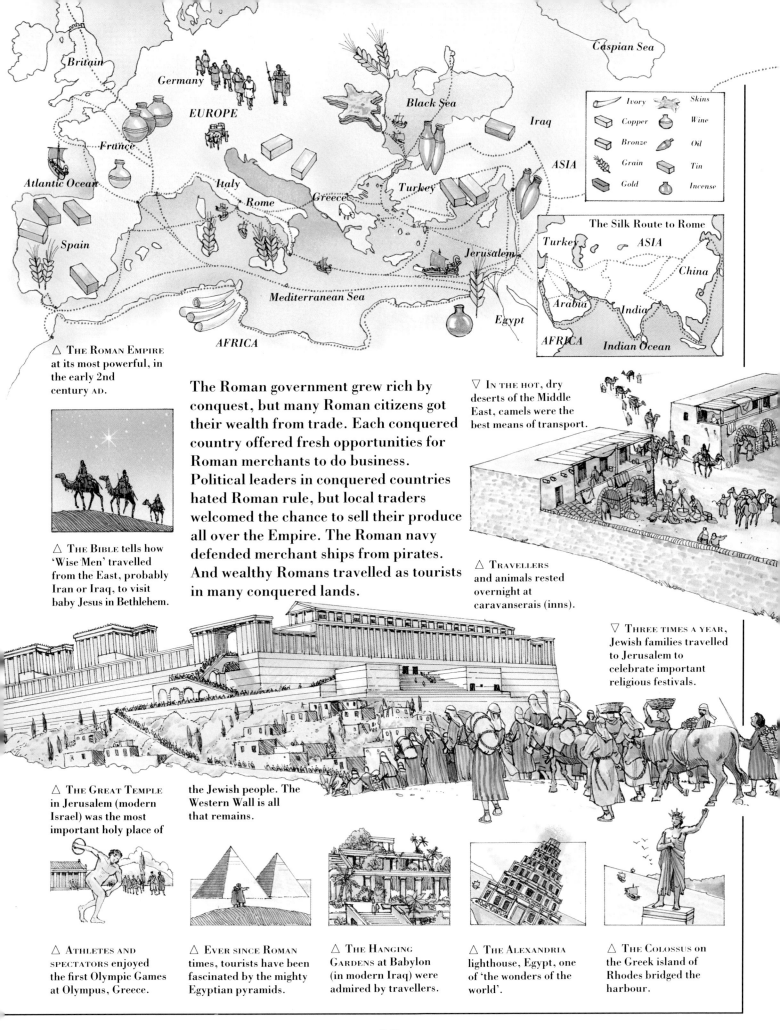

The map

Britain
Germany
EUROPE
France
Atlantic Ocean
Spain
Italy
Rome
Greece
Mediterranean Sea
AFRICA
Black Sea
Iraq
ASIA
Turkey
Jerusalem
Egypt
Caspian Sea

Ivory	Skins
Copper	Wine
Bronze	Oil
Grain	Tin
Gold	Incense

The Silk Route to Rome
Turkey
ASIA
China
Arabia
India
AFRICA
Indian Ocean

△ THE ROMAN EMPIRE at its most powerful, in the early 2nd century AD.

△ THE BIBLE tells how 'Wise Men' travelled from the East, probably Iran or Iraq, to visit baby Jesus in Bethlehem.

The Roman government grew rich by conquest, but many Roman citizens got their wealth from trade. Each conquered country offered fresh opportunities for Roman merchants to do business. Political leaders in conquered countries hated Roman rule, but local traders welcomed the chance to sell their produce all over the Empire. The Roman navy defended merchant ships from pirates. And wealthy Romans travelled as tourists in many conquered lands.

▽ IN THE HOT, dry deserts of the Middle East, camels were the best means of transport.

△ TRAVELLERS and animals rested overnight at caravanserais (inns).

▽ THREE TIMES A YEAR, Jewish families travelled to Jerusalem to celebrate important religious festivals.

△ THE GREAT TEMPLE in Jerusalem (modern Israel) was the most important holy place of the Jewish people. The Western Wall is all that remains.

△ ATHLETES AND SPECTATORS enjoyed the first Olympic Games at Olympus, Greece.

△ EVER SINCE ROMAN times, tourists have been fascinated by the mighty Egyptian pyramids.

△ THE HANGING GARDENS at Babylon (in modern Iraq) were admired by travellers.

△ THE ALEXANDRIA lighthouse, Egypt, one of 'the wonders of the world'.

△ THE COLOSSUS on the Greek island of Rhodes bridged the harbour.

△ THE LARGEST CHINESE junks had a crew of 200 men and could carry almost 1000 passengers plus 1000 tonnes of cargo.

ACROSS THE OCEANS

FROM AROUND AD 700, Chinese sailors made the long sea voyage to trade with wealthy cities on the shores of the Indian Ocean and the Persian Gulf. They exchanged silk, tea and pottery for ivory, gold and rhinoceros horn. They also traded in spices and perfumes from India. Seven hundred years later, a Chinese official, Zheng He, led seven expeditions along this route. His master Yongle, the Chinese emperor, sent 317 ships laden with treasure to governments he wanted to befriend. Almost 30,000 men were conscripted to build and sail them. Between 1405–1433, Zheng He and his fleet visited over thirty lands.

◁ CHINA'S MAIN EXPORTS were pottery and fine porcelain. This elegant dish was shipped to Iran around AD 800.

▽ THE VOYAGES of Zheng He, 1405–1433.

△ CHINESE MAP, 15th century AD. Chinese junks may have rounded the Cape of Good Hope to reach the Atlantic.

Cape of Good Hope

Ocean

Ocean

△ CHINESE MERCHANTS traded with the rich kingdom of Zimbabwe between 1300–1450.

Arabia

China

India

Africa

Bay of Bengal

China Sea

Indian Ocean

Almost four-fifths of the Earth's surface is covered by water – shallow coastal seas, frozen ice-caps and deep oceans. The Pacific Ocean, which separates the land-masses of America, Asia and Australia, has been called a 'wilderness of water'. It is enormous (166,240,000 square kilometres), with wild waves, turbulent currents and terrifying storms. But unlike other wildernesses, it is inhabited. There are thousands of isolated islands, where people have lived for centuries.

How did they get there? There is no written evidence to tell us. But from the languages, cultures and traditions of Pacific island peoples, it seems clear that their origins were elsewhere, in the groups of islands known today as New Guinea and the Philippines. Migrants who settled on remote Pacific islands must have travelled enormous distances across the ocean from their original homes. Even though they were expert boat-builders and navigators, it took great courage to set sail. Who knew what lay across the ocean – new land or a watery grave?

△ DOUBLE-HULLED Polynesian canoes, made from tree trunks bound with fibre and powered by paddles and a sail.

▷ MAORI CHIEFS, portrayed in the 19th century, around 1000 years after their ancestors migrated to New Zealand from other Polynesian islands.

◁ THE ISLANDS of the Pacific were settled beween 2000 BC–AD 1000 by two different groups of people: Melanesians from New Guinea and East Asians from the Philippines and islands nearby. They were brave and skilful sailors.

They loaded their canoes with food, plant seeds and breeding animals, then set off in search of new land.

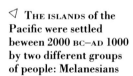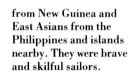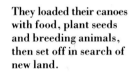

△ HUGE (12 METRE) STONE 'moai' (heads) at Easter Island. Carved between AD 1000–1600, as guardians of the dead. Some scientists think building stopped because the island suffered depopulation and an ecological crisis after all the trees were cut down for fuel and building.

▷ A FEW PEOPLE think the Pacific might have been settled by migrants from America. In 1947, explorer Thor Heyerdahl sailed a balsa-wood raft 6,900 kilometres from Peru to an island near Tahiti, proving that the journey was possible.

THE VIKINGS

△ A BROAD-BEAMED knorr (Viking merchant ship), with a wide hold designed to carry cargo.

THE VIKINGS' HOME was in Scandinavia, in remote north-west Europe. Yet, from there, between around AD 800–1100, they covered vast distances in their graceful, expertly-built ships. Viking raiders swooped across the seas to attack villages in Britain, Ireland, Germany, Italy and France. Viking adventurers journeyed to present-day Turkey to join the Byzantine emperor's army. Viking settlers established new kingdoms in Normandy, Sicily, Dublin and York.

Viking merchants and slave-traders also travelled overland, through bitterly cold Russian forests and along great rivers, to trade with merchants from the Middle East. There was a constant danger of attack from local people, angered by slave trading.

△ A FAST, sleek longship (Viking warship), about 23 metres long. It was powered by the wind or, in a calm, rowed by 32 men. Like all Viking ships it had shallow draft, so it could sail close inshore, letting raiders leap out and attack.

△ BETWEEN THE 8th–11th centuries AD, Viking traders, raiders and settlers travelled throughout Europe, to the Middle East and to Greenland and America. Even though the land was rocky and treeless, Eric the Red called his colony 'Greenland' to encourage new settlers. Around 3,000 Vikings came to live there.

▷ VIKING MERCHANTS bought and sold using silver coins, or bartered (exchanged) goods of equal value.

▽ IN RUSSIA, Viking merchants travelled mainly by river. But part of their route lay overland, so they dragged their boats across country until the next waterway.

▽ VIKING RAIDERS looted Christian churches and monasteries. They knew they would find gold and silver crosses and other treasures there.

△ THE VIKINGS traded amber, timber, fish, furs and slaves from their northern homelands for wine, silks and spices from southern Europe and the Middle East.

◁ ARMED WITH long swords and battleaxes, the Vikings were fierce fighters. They slaughtered their enemies, or captured them to sell as slaves. One British monk wrote this prayer: 'From the terror of the Norsemen, Good Lord deliver us.'

The Vikings also sailed westwards, in search of new land. As their population grew, there was a danger that they would run short of food. In AD 860, Gardar Svarsson's ship was blown by a storm to Iceland. He explored the island, and returned home with tales of rich pasture and plentiful fish. Before long, Vikings had set up a colony there.

In AD 930, another stormy voyage led to the first Viking landing on Greenland. This cold, treeless country was not settled until a Norwegian, Eric the Red, was exiled there as a punishment in AD 982. After his exile was over, he encouraged Viking colonists to return with him. The first village was founded in AD 986.

In the same year, a Viking named Bjarni Herjulfsson set sail from Iceland, but became lost in dense fog. When it cleared, he could see land. But it was not Iceland or Greenland – it was the coast of North America. Bjarni told others about his discovery, and in AD 1000 Leif Eriksson (son of Eric the Red) set out on Bjarni's route. He reached America, making camp at Vinland (modern Newfoundland). But the settlement was abandoned after a few years.

△ YOUNG WOMEN and children captured by Viking raiders fetched high prices as slaves. Old people were not worth much.

▽ IN 1002, Thorwald, Leif Eriksson's brother, attacked a group of Native Americans in Vinland. Their comrades fought back and Thorwald was killed.

▷ SOME VIKINGS died away from home. They left memorial stones, carved with pictures of their ships, like this one from Gotland on the Baltic Sea.

MARCO POLO

R ARE, EXOTIC OBJECTS are always
valuable. From Roman times until the
Middle Ages, silks, spices and porcelain were
among the most precious goods in Europe. None could be
produced locally; all had to be imported.

Merchants who supplied these valuable goods became rich.
But it was a risky business. They had to rely on a network of
trading partners travelling bandit-infested trackways – the
'Silk Route' – which stretched half-way round the world. No
trader made the whole journey himself; he could not cross
frontiers between warring states. However, in 1215, Mongol
armies conquered China, and, by 1223, patrolled the Silk
Route across Asia. The Mongols were brutal, but they
brought peace, and so a few brave travellers set out to explore.

Missionary John de Carpini was the first, in 1245. He was
soon followed by merchants, like Venetian brothers
Niccolo and Maffeo Polo. They left
Venice for China in 1260, returning
triumphantly in 1269. In 1271
they set out again, taking
Niccolo's son, Marco.
Marco worked as roving
ambassador (and maybe
spy) for the Mongol
ruler, Kublai Khan.

△ THE POLOS sailed
from Venice – the
richest trading city in
Europe. Its merchants
specialised in buying
and selling silks from the
East.

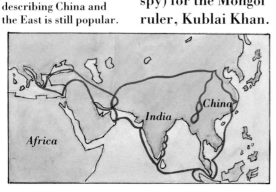

△ MARCO POLO
(1254–1324), one of the
world's best-known
explorers. His book
describing China and
the East is still popular.

△ MARCO POLO'S
TRAVELS. Marco left
Europe in 1271, aged
16. On his journeys, he
explored China, India,
Malaysia and Central
Asia before returning
home to Venice in 1295.

◁ MARCO POLO claimed
he had met a merchant
who had seen dog-
headed cannibals in the
Andaman Islands to the
east of India. These
islands were important
sources of the spices
traded by merchants
like the Polos.

△ MEDIEVAL TRAVEL
was slow and dangerous,
by land or by sea. It
took Marco Polo 4 years
to reach Cambaluc
(modern Beijing) from
Venice. Travellers
journeyed in groups,
carrying food, water
and gifts to use as
bribes. They employed
armed bodyguards to
protect them from
bandits and thieves.

▽ MERCHANTS FROM
Middle Eastern lands
imported spices from
India and South-East
Asia by sea, sailing in
Chinese junks and Arab
dhows (page 21).

Cinnamon

△ AT ACRE (in modern Israel) the Polos met the Pope, who gave them a letter to take to Kublai Khan.

△ THE POLOS sailed along the Persian Gulf, then they continued overland, scorched by hot desert winds.

△ THEIR ROUTE passed through the Pamirs: rugged, wild, uninhabited mountains. It was bitterly cold.

△ IN 1275, the Polos reached Kublai Khan's summer palace at Shengdu. He questioned them about their travels.

△ MARCO MET Chinese merchants and struck bargains using paper money – still unknown in Europe.

△ MARCO ADMIRED the city of Kinsai (Hangzhou), saying it was larger, richer and more beautiful than any in Europe.

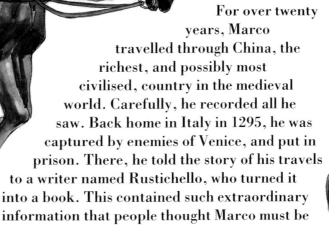

For over twenty years, Marco travelled through China, the richest, and possibly most civilised, country in the medieval world. Carefully, he recorded all he saw. Back home in Italy in 1295, he was captured by enemies of Venice, and put in prison. There, he told the story of his travels to a writer named Rustichello, who turned it into a book. This contained such extraordinary information that people thought Marco must be exaggerating. But, when urged to confess these 'lies' as he lay dying, Marco swore that he had told the truth.

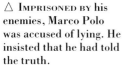

△ IMPRISONED BY his enemies, Marco Polo was accused of lying. He insisted that he had told the truth.

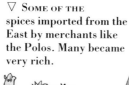

▽ SOME OF THE spices imported from the East by merchants like the Polos. Many became very rich.

Nutmeg

Pepper

Cloves

Silk Route

Central Asia

China

Africa

Arabia

India

△ CRAFTWORKERS IN China and the Middle East kept secret the skills they used to make fine goods like these for sale in Europe.

MUSLIMS

THE FIRST MUSLIM communities lived and worshipped in the cities of Medina and Mecca, in Arabia, in the early seventh century AD. But within 200 years, their Islamic faith had spread far beyond the Middle East. A new, international civilisation began to develop as the teachings of Islam mingled with local customs and traditions in many parts of the world. Soldiers, administrators, scholars, preachers and traders travelled through the Muslim lands; they found a shared faith and a common system of laws. Increasingly, Arabic was spoken by educated Muslims, wherever they lived. Thousands of Muslim pilgrims travelled each year to the holy city of Mecca. It was a religious duty, but also a time to make new friends and business deals.

All these contacts helped create an awareness of the wider world among many Muslim people. Muslim geographers and explorers were respected and admired.

△ IBN FADLAN observed a dramatic Viking funeral ceremony on his travels through icy northern Russia.

△ THE BEDOUIN people of Arabia travelled the desert to find water and grazing for their flocks.

▷ THE ARABS were skilled astronomers, and they used their knowledge of the night sky to help them navigate across the vast Arabian desert, with its shifting sand-dunes and confusing mirages. Instruments like this astrolabe (invented around AD 700) helped measure the position of the stars.

△ GEOGRAPHER AL IDRISI's map of the world was engraved on a huge silver disk. Sadly, it was later destroyed in a fire.

▷ ALL MUSLIMS aim to make a pilgrimage (called a 'hajj') to Mecca at least once during their lifetime. In past centuries, pilgrimages could take many months.

◁ THE KAABA (a cube-shaped building), the most sacred shrine in the heart of the holy city of Mecca, Arabia. It is kept covered by beautiful gold embroideries.

Spain

Malaga

Morocco

AFRICA

Timbuktu

Djénné

Niani

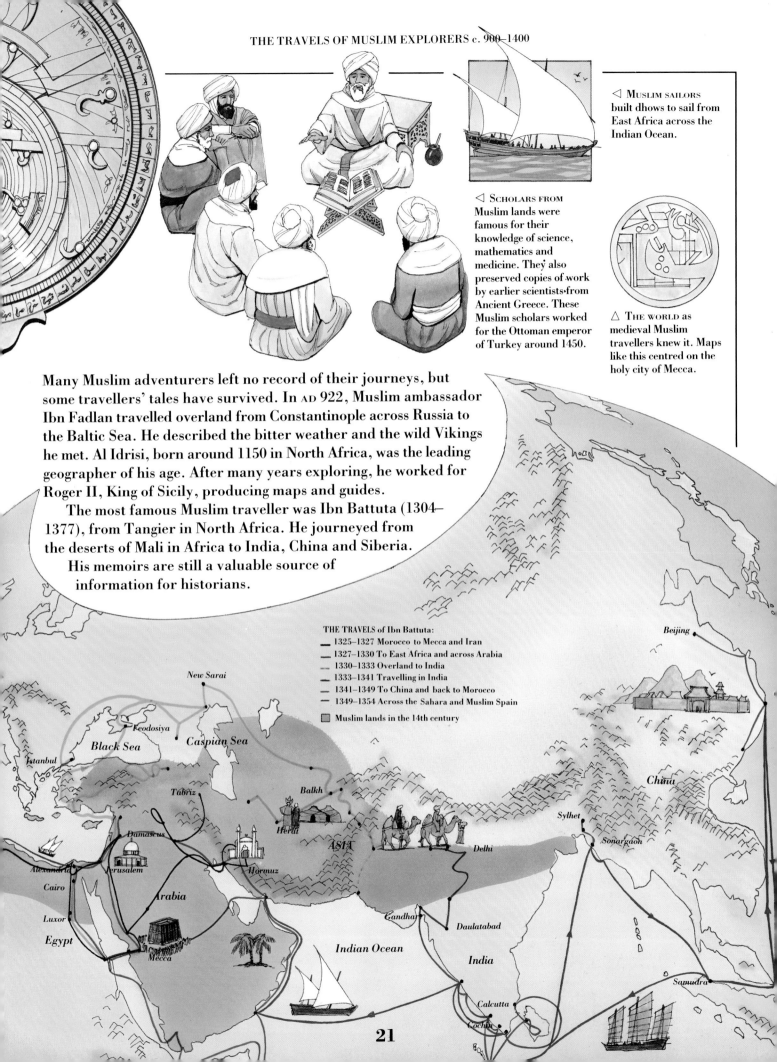

◁ **MUSLIM SAILORS** built dhows to sail from East Africa across the Indian Ocean.

◁ **SCHOLARS FROM** Muslim lands were famous for their knowledge of science, mathematics and medicine. They also preserved copies of work by earlier scientists from Ancient Greece. These Muslim scholars worked for the Ottoman emperor of Turkey around 1450.

△ **THE WORLD** as medieval Muslim travellers knew it. Maps like this centred on the holy city of Mecca.

Many Muslim adventurers left no record of their journeys, but some travellers' tales have survived. In AD 922, Muslim ambassador Ibn Fadlan travelled overland from Constantinople across Russia to the Baltic Sea. He described the bitter weather and the wild Vikings he met. Al Idrisi, born around 1150 in North Africa, was the leading geographer of his age. After many years exploring, he worked for Roger II, King of Sicily, producing maps and guides.

The most famous Muslim traveller was Ibn Battuta (1304–1377), from Tangier in North Africa. He journeyed from the deserts of Mali in Africa to India, China and Siberia. His memoirs are still a valuable source of information for historians.

THE TRAVELS of Ibn Battuta:
— 1325–1327 Morocco to Mecca and Iran
— 1327–1330 To East Africa and across Arabia
— 1330–1333 Overland to India
— 1333–1341 Travelling in India
— 1341–1349 To China and back to Morocco
— 1349–1354 Across the Sahara and Muslim Spain
☐ Muslim lands in the 14th century

Beijing

New Sarai

Feodosiya

Black Sea

Caspian Sea

China

Istanbul

Tabriz

Balkh

Sylhet

Herat

Sonargaon

Damascus

ASIA

Delhi

Jerusalem

Alexandria

Hormuz

Cairo

Arabia

Gandhar

Luxor

Daulatabad

Egypt

Mecca

Indian Ocean

India

Samudra

Calcutta

Cochin

AFRICA AND AMERICA

△ PORTUGUESE MAP, drawn in 1489, showing the area of the world known to European sailors and scholars.

PRINCE HENRY THE NAVIGATOR of Portugal was ambitious – but poor. How could he win fame and fortune? After an exciting expedition to fight in North Africa, he decided to investigate other more distant lands, by sponsoring yearly voyages of exploration from 1418 until his death in 1460. Prince Henry's sailors discovered remote Atlantic islands (Madeira, Cape Verde, the Azores) and sailed over 2,000 miles along the coast of West Africa. Their enterprise won rich rewards; they traded profitably with African nations supplying sugar, gold, ivory and, tragically, slaves.

After Prince Henry's death, Portuguese rulers continued to encourage contacts with Africa. In 1488, Bartolomeu Dias rounded the Cape of Good Hope – a return trip of almost 15,000 miles. His voyage proved there was a sea route to India. It also encouraged those explorers, like Christopher Columbus, who believed the world was round. He argued that he could reach the fabulous eastern kingdoms described in Marco Polo's book by sailing west.

△ PRINCE HENRY the Navigator of Portugal (1394–1460) encouraged explorers' voyages.

◁ VASCO DA GAMA (c.1469–1524) was the first European to sail round Africa and reach India, 1497–1499.

△ MAGNETIC COMPASS, made around 1500.

◁ QUEEN ISABELLA and King Ferdinand, joint rulers of Spain, funded Columbus's voyage, 1492.

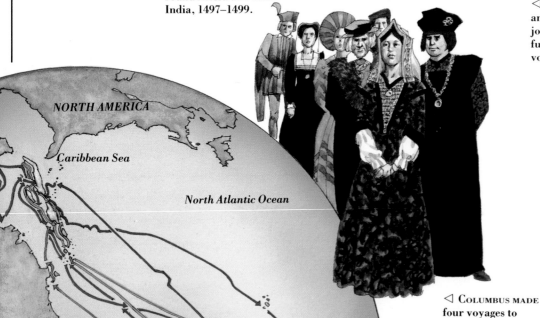

NORTH AMERICA

Caribbean Sea

North Atlantic Ocean

SOUTH AMERICA

South Atlantic Ocean

SPAIN

AFRICA

◁ COLUMBUS MADE four voyages to America:

■	1492–1493
■	1493–1496
□	1498–1500
■	1502–1504

△ COLUMBUS'S SHIP *Niña*: 20 metres long and 7 metres wide, with its original sails.

△ COLUMBUS'S second ship, the *Pinta*.

△ COLUMBUS BROUGHT new foods from America: sweet potatoes and pineapples.

△ THE COAT OF ARMS granted to Columbus by the Spanish royal family after his epic voyage.

▽ MOCTEZUMA, LEADER of the Aztec people, first met the Spanish explorer and conqueror Cortes in 1519. Their interpreter was a Native American woman, Malintzin (or 'Doña Marina').

△ COLUMBUS'S SHIP *Santa Maria*. Columbus's ships were specially fitted with square sails instead of the triangular lateen sails normally used by Mediterranean vessels. Square sails could better withstand the fierce Atlantic gales.

It took many years for Columbus to find patrons to pay for his voyage. But in 1492, he landed in America (the Bahama Islands), thinking it was Japan. Columbus refused to believe he had discovered a new continent, but other Europeans quickly saw opportunities in this 'New World'. The name they gave it betrays their attitude; they cared nothing for its inhabitants. The Spaniard Hernan Cortes conquered the Aztecs of Mexico between 1519–1521. In a few years, ninety per cent of them were dead.

▽ SIR FRANCIS DRAKE (1540–1596), the English explorer.

▷ DRAKE HARRIED the great galleons bringing the treasures of the New World back to Spain. The Spanish called him a pirate, but to the English he was a hero.

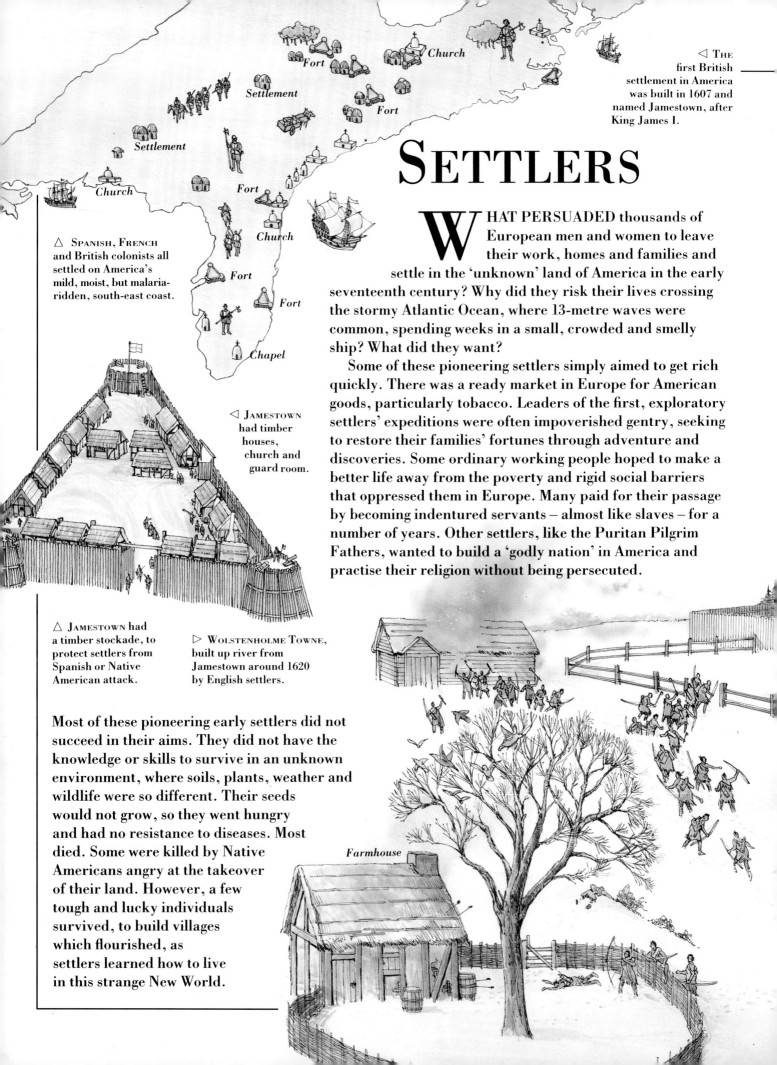

Church

Fort

Settlement

Fort

Settlement

Church

Fort

Church

Fort

Fort

Chapel

◁ The first British settlement in America was built in 1607 and named Jamestown, after King James I.

△ SPANISH, FRENCH and British colonists all settled on America's mild, moist, but malaria-ridden, south-east coast.

◁ JAMESTOWN had timber houses, church and guard room.

SETTLERS

WHAT PERSUADED thousands of European men and women to leave their work, homes and families and settle in the 'unknown' land of America in the early seventeenth century? Why did they risk their lives crossing the stormy Atlantic Ocean, where 13-metre waves were common, spending weeks in a small, crowded and smelly ship? What did they want?

Some of these pioneering settlers simply aimed to get rich quickly. There was a ready market in Europe for American goods, particularly tobacco. Leaders of the first, exploratory settlers' expeditions were often impoverished gentry, seeking to restore their families' fortunes through adventure and discoveries. Some ordinary working people hoped to make a better life away from the poverty and rigid social barriers that oppressed them in Europe. Many paid for their passage by becoming indentured servants – almost like slaves – for a number of years. Other settlers, like the Puritan Pilgrim Fathers, wanted to build a 'godly nation' in America and practise their religion without being persecuted.

△ JAMESTOWN had a timber stockade, to protect settlers from Spanish or Native American attack.

▷ WOLSTENHOLME TOWNE, built up river from Jamestown around 1620 by English settlers.

Most of these pioneering early settlers did not succeed in their aims. They did not have the knowledge or skills to survive in an unknown environment, where soils, plants, weather and wildlife were so different. Their seeds would not grow, so they went hungry and had no resistance to diseases. Most died. Some were killed by Native Americans angry at the takeover of their land. However, a few tough and lucky individuals survived, to build villages which flourished, as settlers learned how to live in this strange New World.

Farmhouse

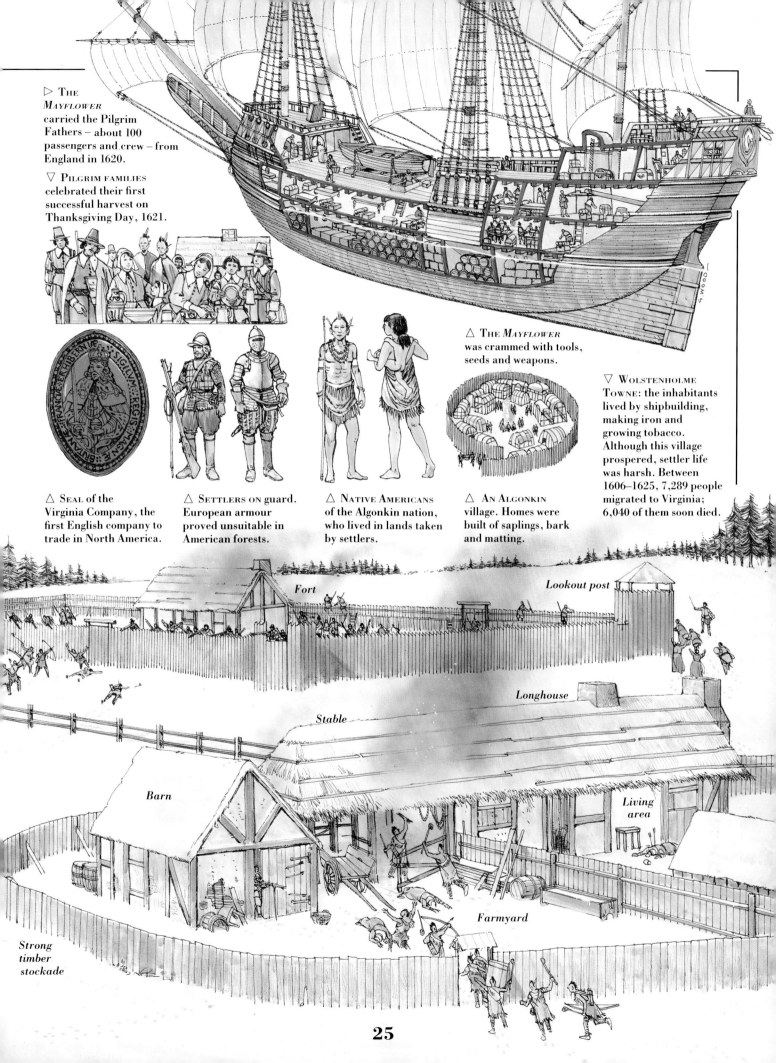

▷ THE *MAYFLOWER* carried the Pilgrim Fathers – about 100 passengers and crew – from England in 1620.

▽ PILGRIM FAMILIES celebrated their first successful harvest on Thanksgiving Day, 1621.

△ THE *MAYFLOWER* was crammed with tools, seeds and weapons.

▽ WOLSTENHOLME TOWNE: the inhabitants lived by shipbuilding, making iron and growing tobacco. Although this village prospered, settler life was harsh. Between 1606–1625, 7,289 people migrated to Virginia; 6,040 of them soon died.

△ SEAL of the Virginia Company, the first English company to trade in North America.

△ SETTLERS ON GUARD. European armour proved unsuitable in American forests.

△ NATIVE AMERICANS of the Algonkin nation, who lived in lands taken by settlers.

△ AN ALGONKIN village. Homes were built of saplings, bark and matting.

Fort

Lookout post

Longhouse

Stable

Barn

Living area

Farmyard

Strong timber stockade

THE PACIFIC

DURING THE FIFTEENTH and sixteenth centuries, heroic voyages of exploration led to tremendous advances in geographical knowledge and understanding. In 1492, Columbus landed in America. In 1497, Cabot – like the Vikings – reached Newfoundland. In 1497–1499, Vasco da Gama sailed round Africa to India. In 1519–1522, Magellan and Cano made the first voyage right round the globe. The Dutch explorer Tasman sighted Australia and New Zealand in 1642. But now, in the mid-eighteenth century, two mysteries remained unsolved.

Asia

Africa

North America

Australia

South America

Antarctica

CAPTAIN COOK   SEAMAN   SURGEON   BOTANIST   COOK   MASTER MATE

△ THE THREE VOYAGES of Captain Cook:
1768–1771
1772–1775
1776–1780

ARTIST   ARTIST   BOATSWAIN   CARPENTER   MARINE

△ THE CREW of Cook's *Endeavour*, was made up of British Navy officers (who took charge), marines (who kept discipline and protected the ship from attack) and ordinary sailors (who manned the sails and rigging). There were also artists, scientists and servants.

△ ON HIS first voyage, off the coast of New Zealand, Cook clashed with Maori warriors, who shouted a traditional 'challenge to war' from their canoes.

◁ PAGES FROM a sketchbook kept by one of Cook's artists, Sydney Parkinson. He made over 1,500 drawings of Pacific plants and animals.

Was there a 'north-west passage' – a sea-route running north of Canada to Asia? And was there a great southern continent hidden beyond Africa and Asia? A British naval officer, Captain James Cook, felt sure these questions could be answered by scientifically exploring the vast Pacific Ocean. Directed by leading scientists, he made three voyages between 1768–1779. First, he sailed to Australia, then onwards, around the world. Next, he sailed south towards the Antarctic, proving there was no southern continent. On his third voyage, like many others before and since, Cook did not find the north-west passage – because it is frozen for much of the year.

▷ THE *ENDEAVOUR* was originally a coal-carrying ship. Cook chose it because it was strongly built and had room for 600 tonnes of cargo and crew.

◁ COOK'S SCIENTISTS also collected specimens, including dried flowers, seeds and animal skins.

In spite of this failure, Cook's voyages proved immensely important because of the detailed scientific notes and drawings he and his colleagues made of the places they visited. He also made observations of the southern stars, invisible in the northern hemisphere.

Cook's scientific approach also benefited his crew. He insisted they ate a healthy diet, including fresh fruit and vegetables. He ordered that the ship should be kept very clean, to prevent infestation by rats, lice and other disease-carrying creatures.

Stores

Fresh water

Living quarters

Wardroom

◁ DR JAMES LIND (1716–1794), who pioneered treatment of scurvy, caused by lack of Vitamin C.

▽ COOK'S chronometer kept going for his journey round the world, enabling him to calculate his position of longitude accurately.

△ COOK KEPT his ship's medicine chest well supplied with simple remedies.

◁ COOK'S PORTABLE observatory, for studying the stars.

▽ COOK'S THIRD voyage: *Resolution* and *Discovery* anchored off the north-west coast of Canada, 1778.

27

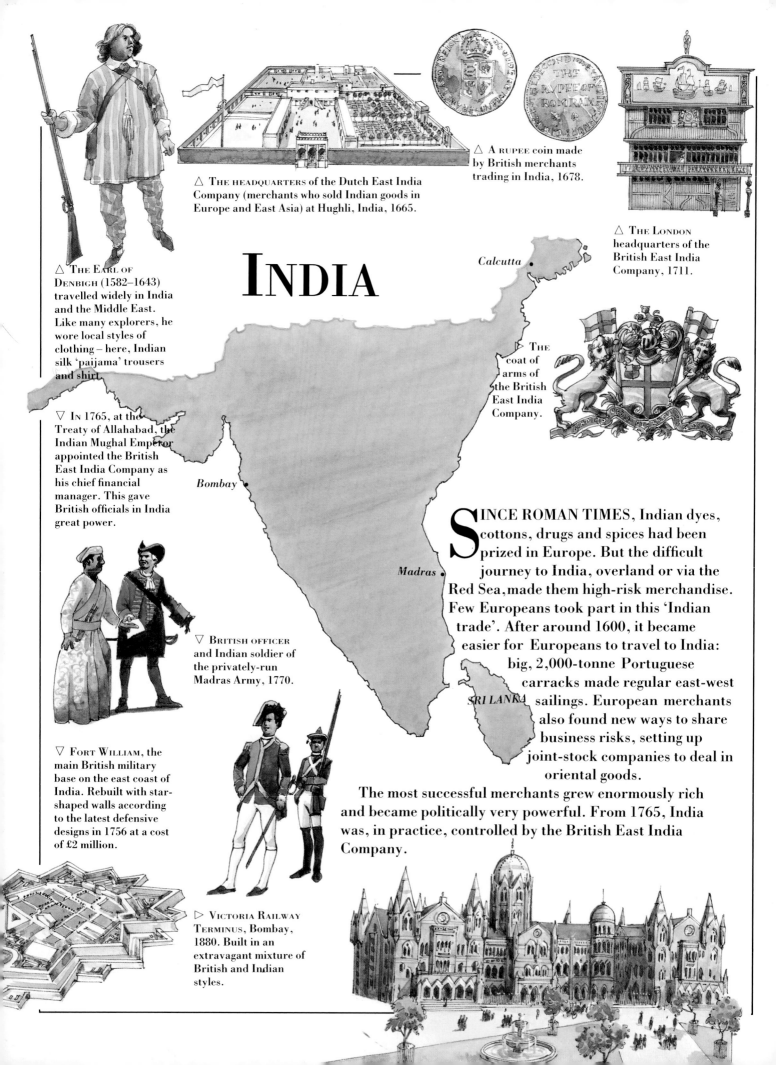

INDIA

△ THE HEADQUARTERS of the Dutch East India Company (merchants who sold Indian goods in Europe and East Asia) at Hughli, India, 1665.

△ A RUPEE coin made by British merchants trading in India, 1678.

△ THE LONDON headquarters of the British East India Company, 1711.

△ THE EARL OF DENBIGH (1582–1643) travelled widely in India and the Middle East. Like many explorers, he wore local styles of clothing – here, Indian silk 'paijama' trousers and shirt.

▽ IN 1765, at the Treaty of Allahabad, the Indian Mughal Emperor appointed the British East India Company as his chief financial manager. This gave British officials in India great power.

▷ THE coat of arms of the British East India Company.

Calcutta

Bombay

Madras

SRI LANKA

▽ BRITISH OFFICER and Indian soldier of the privately-run Madras Army, 1770.

▽ FORT WILLIAM, the main British military base on the east coast of India. Rebuilt with star-shaped walls according to the latest defensive designs in 1756 at a cost of £2 million.

▷ VICTORIA RAILWAY TERMINUS, Bombay, 1880. Built in an extravagant mixture of British and Indian styles.

SINCE ROMAN TIMES, Indian dyes, cottons, drugs and spices had been prized in Europe. But the difficult journey to India, overland or via the Red Sea, made them high-risk merchandise. Few Europeans took part in this 'Indian trade'. After around 1600, it became easier for Europeans to travel to India: big, 2,000-tonne Portuguese carracks made regular east-west sailings. European merchants also found new ways to share business risks, setting up joint-stock companies to deal in oriental goods.

The most successful merchants grew enormously rich and became politically very powerful. From 1765, India was, in practice, controlled by the British East India Company.

CHINA

F**OR CENTURIES**, under the rule of the Qing Dynasty (1636–1911), the ancient land of Cathay (modern China) was closed to travellers from overseas. The Chinese government did not welcome foreigners. Even unarmed missionary priests were watched.

The same was true for Central Asia – the vast, bleak region between China, Russia, Turkey and Iran. It was governed by the tsars of Russia and the Ottoman emperors. They, too, were suspicious of outsiders. And so, during the seventeenth and eighteenth centuries, when European travellers were investigating other parts of the world, 'far Cathay' remained largely unexplored by them.

◁ **Jesuit missionary** priests, like Father Matteo Ricci (1552– 1610), were among the first Europeans to explore China, studying the Chinese language and way of life.

△ **Francis Younghusband** and his companions took immense risks when they ventured into the unknown in 1886. Younghusband had never even seen a desert before he began his journey.

△ **Map of 'Tartary'** (Central Asia) made by Anthony Jenkinson after his return to England in 1562.

△ **Sven Hedin** (1865– 1952), Swedish explorer and map-maker, spent over 40 years travelling in the harsh deserts of Central Asia. Hedin was almost buried in a sandstorm and nearly died from thirst on his first major expedition in the Takla Makan desert, 1893. All his companions perished.

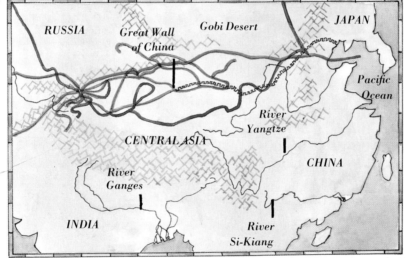

◁ **Routes pioneered** by explorers in Central Asia:
- Francis Younghusband, 1886
- Sven Hedin, 1893– 1936
- Sir Aurel Stein, 1900–1930

In the nineteenth century, the situation changed. Central Asia became the setting for 'the Great Game', the rivalry between Britain and Russia to control the northern routes to India. Travel became possible. Explorers faced bandits, haunted deserts, howling sandstorms, extreme temperatures and deadly bubonic plague. But men like Sven Hedin and Aurel Stein were rewarded by discovering the remains of vanished civilisations.

▷ **Wall-painting** (7th century AD) preserved by the dry desert atmosphere near Khotan on the western borders of China, discovered by Hungarian/British archaeologist and explorer Sir Aurel Stein (1862–1943).

AFRICA

△ Map drawn by the 16th-century French geographer, Descalier. The coastline is based on accurate reports by sailors.

Nineteenth-century travel-writers often described Africa as 'the dark continent'. Today, such a description would be thought offensive, but few of those early writers were commenting on colour or race. They were trying to convey a sense of mystery and danger. For centuries, there had been close trading contacts between Arab, Indian and European travellers and African merchants living north of the Sahara and along the east and west coasts. But, in the early nineteenth century, the vast interior of the African continent was almost unknown to the outside world.

△ The French Emperor Napoleon fought in Egypt in 1798–1799. His visit gave him a lifelong interest in ancient Egypt.

△ In spite of campaigns in Europe, the trade in slaves to America flourished in many African lands.

△ Mungo Park (1771–1806), a young Scottish doctor, was the first European scientifically to explore the Niger river in West Africa. He was drowned in an ambush there.

△ European explorers disguised themselves as Arab merchants to study African Muslim ways of life.

▽ In 1858, Samuel Baker and his wife travelled in Africa with 90 servants and a dismantled steam-boat.

△ Richard Burton (1821–1890) was a brilliant linguist, speaking 29 languages. Together with John Speke (1827–1864, *right*), he made a hazardous journey in 1858 to seek the source of the Nile.

△ Gazelle, from Speke's sketchbook.

This ignorance about Africa was mainly the result of its geography and climate. Depending on location, temperature and rainfall, the African landscape was thickly covered either with jungle or with coarse, scrubby thornbush and tall, wiry grass. There were high mountains, deep valleys and rocky ravines. All this made travel extremely difficult. Even the rivers, usually the easiest routes if there are no roads, were full of waterfalls and rapids, making them impassable. Insects had poisonous stings or carried dangerous diseases; some fevers could kill within 24 hours. And travellers in regions where the local peoples were at war might well be arrested and killed in case they were spies.

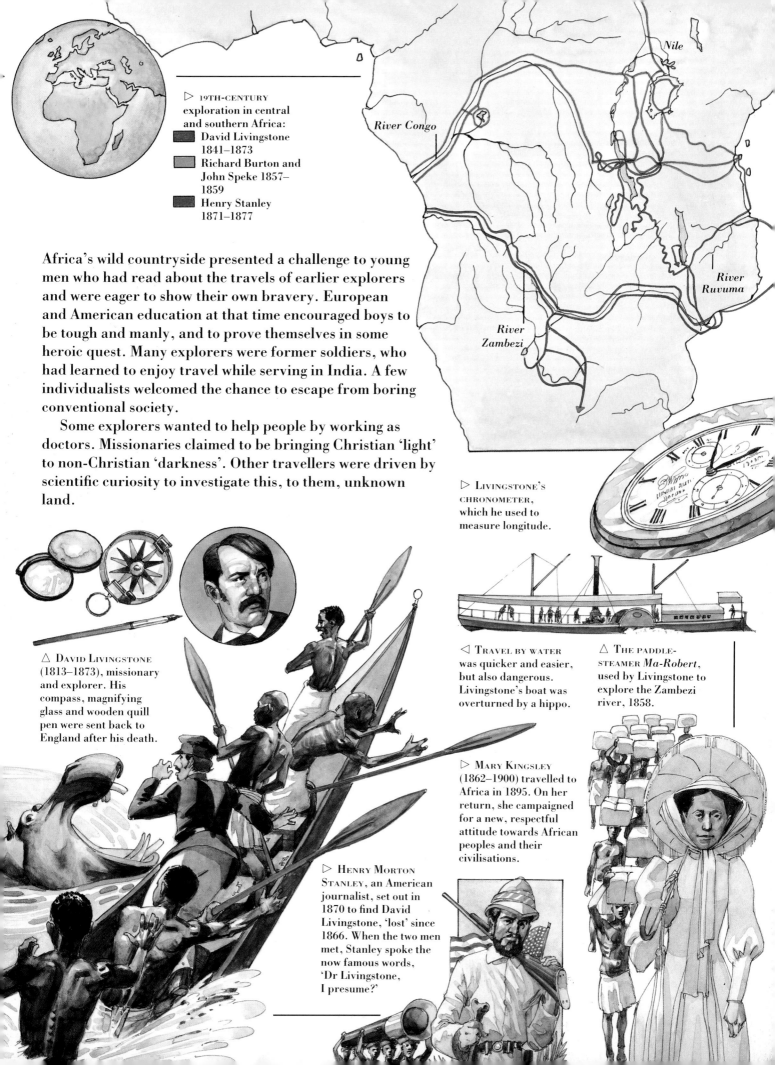

▷ 19TH-CENTURY exploration in central and southern Africa:
David Livingstone 1841–1873
Richard Burton and John Speke 1857–1859
Henry Stanley 1871–1877

Africa's wild countryside presented a challenge to young men who had read about the travels of earlier explorers and were eager to show their own bravery. European and American education at that time encouraged boys to be tough and manly, and to prove themselves in some heroic quest. Many explorers were former soldiers, who had learned to enjoy travel while serving in India. A few individualists welcomed the chance to escape from boring conventional society.

Some explorers wanted to help people by working as doctors. Missionaries claimed to be bringing Christian 'light' to non-Christian 'darkness'. Other travellers were driven by scientific curiosity to investigate this, to them, unknown land.

Nile

River Congo

River Ruvuma

River Zambezi

▷ LIVINGSTONE'S CHRONOMETER, which he used to measure longitude.

△ DAVID LIVINGSTONE (1813–1873), missionary and explorer. His compass, magnifying glass and wooden quill pen were sent back to England after his death.

◁ TRAVEL BY WATER was quicker and easier, but also dangerous. Livingstone's boat was overturned by a hippo.

△ THE PADDLE-STEAMER *Ma-Robert*, used by Livingstone to explore the Zambezi river, 1858.

▷ MARY KINGSLEY (1862–1900) travelled to Africa in 1895. On her return, she campaigned for a new, respectful attitude towards African peoples and their civilisations.

▷ HENRY MORTON STANLEY, an American journalist, set out in 1870 to find David Livingstone, 'lost' since 1866. When the two men met, Stanley spoke the now famous words, 'Dr Livingstone, I presume?'

OVERLAND

THE FIRST EUROPEAN settlement in the Americas was established in 1593, at Hispaniola in the Caribbean. For almost 200 years most new settlements were on the east coast of North America or the banks of rivers. It made sense to settle close to ports and other Europeans.

△ EUROPEAN TRACKERS and fur-trappers hunted wild animals and traded furs in North American forests.

△ MERCHANTS' ASSOCIATIONS, like the Hudson's Bay Company of Canada, built well-defended trading posts; this is Fort Garry. Forts developed into towns and became bases for further exploration.

△ CANADIAN RIVERS were full of dangerous rapids. But portage (carrying canoes across country) was slow and exhausting work. In 1793, Mackenzie and his team found the forests so dense and the ground so rocky that it took 10 hours to travel 3 miles.

The Native American inhabitants either migrated westwards or were driven out in the bloody Indian Wars (1622–1763).

But some European Americans wanted to know what lay beyond the coastal regions. Merchants and fur-trappers who worked in the great forests were told by Native Americans of limitless prairies and spectacular mountain ranges 'way out west'. Other explorers were motivated by national pride: there was fierce rivalry between Britain, France and Spain.

The expedition led by Captains Lewis and Clark, which crossed the entire continent, was funded by the US government after it acquired new territories from France in 1803.

Arctic Ocean

Alaska

Greenland

Hudson Bay

Newfoundland

EARLY EXPLORERS IN NORTH AMERICA:

Cartier 1534
Champlain 1608
Brulé 1608–1621
Nicolet 1634
de la Salle 1681
Vérendrye 1728
Mackenzie 1789
Mackenzie 1792–1793
Lewis and Clark 1804–1806

◁ ALEXANDER MACKENZIE, a young Scottish trader, made two major expeditions to explore the Canadian interior. In 1789, he set out for the Pacific coast, but reached the Arctic Ocean. In 1792, he travelled westwards, finally reaching the Pacific in 1793. Mackenzie travelled through wild and almost uninhabited countryside. He kept careful notes, marvelling at the beautiful scenery and plentiful wildlife he saw.

△ CAPTAIN MERIWETHER LEWIS (1774–1809), soldier, explorer and Governor of Louisiana.

△ CAPTAIN WILLIAM CLARK (1770–1838). Together with Lewis, he made the first crossing of America.

THE PROBLEMS facing anyone trying to cross Australia were even worse than those facing explorers of North America. The interior of Australia is mostly scorching, shadeless desert, with little food and less water.

△ ROBERT BURKE (1820–1861, *left*) and William Wills (1834–1861, *right*). Together, they made the first north-south crossing of Australia. They died of starvation and exhaustion on the return journey.

△ SERGEANT PATRICK GRASS, of the Lewis and Clark expedition, kept an illustrated journal. His pictures show (*left*) a meeting with Native Americans and (*right*) an accident on the river.

▷ EXPLORERS in Australia were often helped by Aboriginal people, who were excellent trackers. Without them, the explorers would have died. Unlike the Aboriginals, the explorers lacked the skills to find food and water in the desert.

◁ LATER IN the 19th century, settlers and gold prospectors followed dangerous cross-country trails to the 'Wild West' of America.

Captain Cook visited Australia in 1770 and reported good farming land near Sydney. The first settlers found he was wrong. They needed farmland, but the Great Dividing Range of mountains barred the way. In 1813, explorers Blaxland, Lawson and Wentworth discovered a way across the mountains and fertile land on the far side. This was fine for the farmers, but the British government wanted explorers to go further to secure British rule.

Over the next seventy-five years many explorers attempting to cross Australia died or went mad in the heat.

▽ THE FIRST European explorers in Australia faced searing desert heat. Charles Sturt recorded a temperature of 119°F (31°C) in 1845. He commented: 'The stillness of death reigned around us'.

△ THE 'FRONTIER TOWN' of Adelaide, starting point for many early expeditions into the Australian desert.

▷ AUSTRALIAN EXPLORERS:
- ┅┅┅ Charles Sturt 1829–1844
- ┈┈┈ Ludwig Leichhardt 1844–1845
- ━ ━ ━ Robert Burke and William Wills 1860–1861
- •••• John Stuart 1861–1862
- ·─·─· John and Alexander Forrest 1869–1879
- ━•━•━ Peter Warburton 1873 Ernest Giles 1875–1876

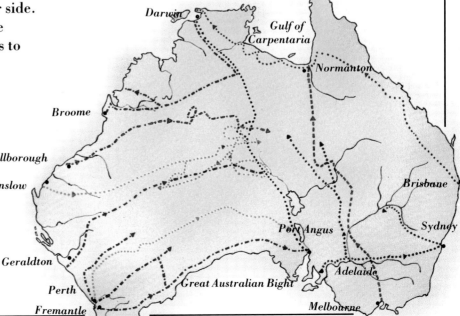

Darwin
Gulf of Carpentaria
Normanton
Broome
Shellborough
Onslow
Brisbane
Geraldton
Port Angus
Sydney
Perth
Great Australian Bight
Adelaide
Fremantle
Melbourne

BELOW THE WAVES

H OW DEEP WAS THE OCEAN? What creatures lived beneath the waves? For centuries, these questions remained unanswered. Although, from around 1500 onwards, navigators and map-makers produced accurate charts showing coastlines, winds and currents, there was no way of exploring underwater, because human beings need fresh air to breathe. Even Japanese women divers, specially-trained since childhood to search oyster-beds for pearls, could only average 1½ minutes underwater, before hurtling, gasping, to the surface. Sailors used weighted lines to 'sound' (measure) the depth of water in shallow seas.

△ HALLEY'S DIVING BELL, 1690, trapped air inside, allowing men to work on the seabed. Extra air was pumped in through leather pipes.

△ THE *CHALLENGER*, the first ship specially fitted out for deep-sea exploration.

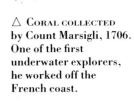

△ CORAL COLLECTED by Count Marsigli, 1706. One of the first underwater explorers, he worked off the French coast.

◁ GERMAN DIVING SUIT, invented by Augustus Siebe in 1819. Air was pumped into the helmet under pressure, keeping sea water out.

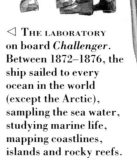

◁ THE LABORATORY on board *Challenger*. Between 1872–1876, the ship sailed to every ocean in the world (except the Arctic), sampling the sea water, studying marine life, mapping coastlines, islands and rocky reefs.

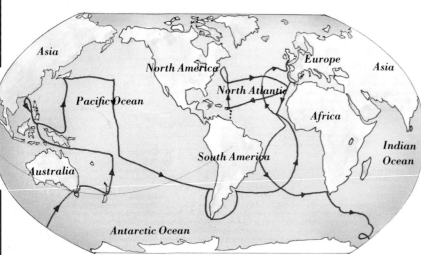

Asia

North America

Pacific Ocean

North Atlantic

Europe

Asia

Africa

South America

Indian Ocean

Australia

Antarctic Ocean

◁ THE VOYAGES made by *Challenger*.

Fishermen sometimes discovered extraordinary-looking fish in their nets. But until the seventeenth century, when explorers invented the trawl dredge and the diving bell, there was no scientific investigation of the sea's depths.

▷ THE DREDGE or beam trawl was invented in the 17th century. It was like a large open sack, submerged to a predetermined depth, which gathered up sea creatures as a boat dragged it along.

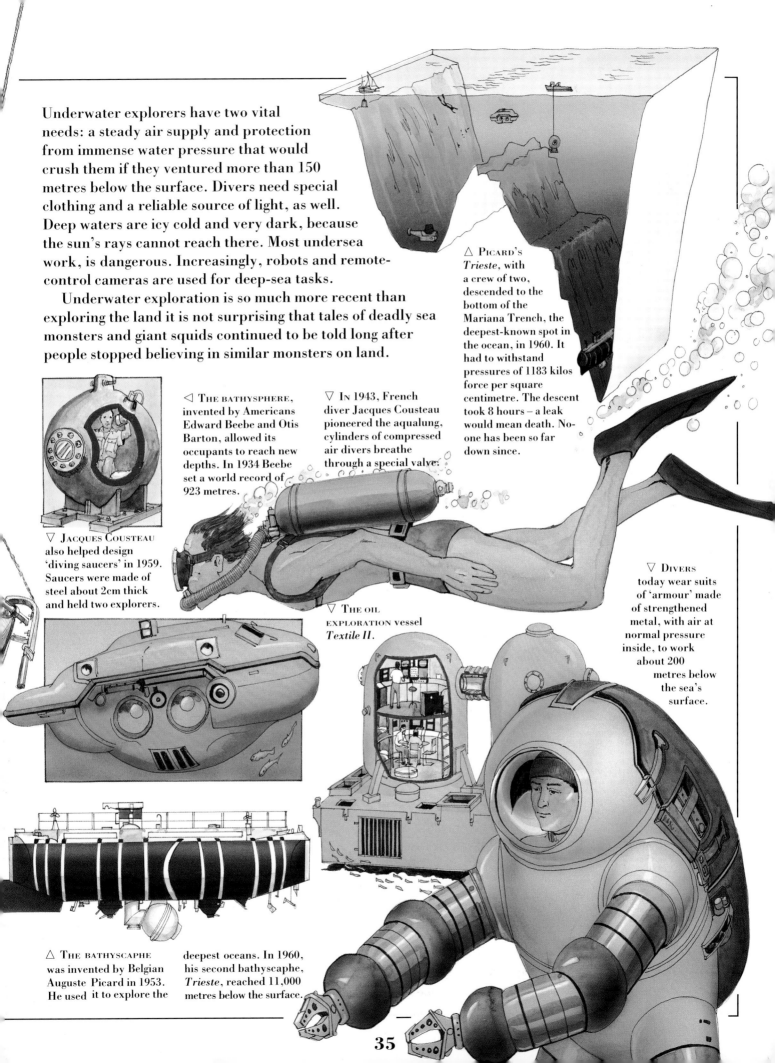

Underwater explorers have two vital needs: a steady air supply and protection from immense water pressure that would crush them if they ventured more than 150 metres below the surface. Divers need special clothing and a reliable source of light, as well. Deep waters are icy cold and very dark, because the sun's rays cannot reach there. Most undersea work, is dangerous. Increasingly, robots and remote-control cameras are used for deep-sea tasks.

Underwater exploration is so much more recent than exploring the land it is not surprising that tales of deadly sea monsters and giant squids continued to be told long after people stopped believing in similar monsters on land.

△ PICARD'S *Trieste*, with a crew of two, descended to the bottom of the Mariana Trench, the deepest-known spot in the ocean, in 1960. It had to withstand pressures of 1183 kilos force per square centimetre. The descent took 8 hours – a leak would mean death. No-one has been so far down since.

◁ THE BATHYSPHERE, invented by Americans Edward Beebe and Otis Barton, allowed its occupants to reach new depths. In 1934 Beebe set a world record of 923 metres.

▽ IN 1943, French diver Jacques Cousteau pioneered the aqualung, cylinders of compressed air divers breathe through a special valve.

▽ JACQUES COUSTEAU also helped design 'diving saucers' in 1959. Saucers were made of steel about 2cm thick and held two explorers.

▽ THE OIL EXPLORATION vessel *Textile II*.

▽ DIVERS today wear suits of 'armour' made of strengthened metal, with air at normal pressure inside, to work about 200 metres below the sea's surface.

△ THE BATHYSCAPHE was invented by Belgian Auguste Picard in 1953. He used it to explore the deepest oceans. In 1960, his second bathyscaphe, *Trieste*, reached 11,000 metres below the surface.

THE POLES

△ THE NORTH POLE is the northernmost point on the earth's surface, a vast expanse of permanently frozen ice, floating in icy seas.

EARLY EXPLORATIONS – Cook's voyages in the Pacific (1766–1780), Barents' expedition to north Norway (1596–1597), Bering's explorations north of Alaska (1728), and the British *Challenger*'s voyage to investigate the oceans (1872) – all meant that, by the late nineteenth century, geographers knew a fair amount about the polar regions. They understood how the ice-caps were formed, kept records of polar weather, and had mapped Arctic and Antarctic boundaries. But no-one had yet managed to reach either the North or the South Pole. Since governments were now beginning to fund scientific explorations, the 'race to the poles' became a matter of national pride.

△ DUTCH SAILOR Willem Barents (died 1597) explored the Arctic oceans. The sea north-east of Norway is named after him.

△ IN 1596, Barents and his crew were trapped as the Arctic seas froze. They struggled ashore, built a cabin from ship's timbers and sheltered through the bitter winter. Barents died on the homeward journey next spring.

▷ CHARLES HALL (1821–1871) was an American publisher who made three unsuccessful attempts to reach the North Pole. He died during his third expedition.

△ HALL PREPARED for his journeys by studying the food, shelters, boats and survival techniques developed by the Inuit peoples who lived in savagely cold Arctic regions. He also learned to drive sledges pulled by hardy Inuit husky dogs.

Most people agree that American Robert Peary won the race to the North Pole, in 1909. But some say he took longer than he claimed. Conditions in the Arctic are so harsh they did not believe he and his companions could really drag heavy sledges over rough ice for 61 kilometres each day, as Peary said. In good conditions, with modern sledges, the record is 37 kilometres in 15 hours.

△ AMERICAN NAVY OFFICER Robert Peary (1856–1920) claimed to be the first man to reach the North Pole, on his eighth attempt, with five companions, in 1909.

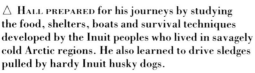

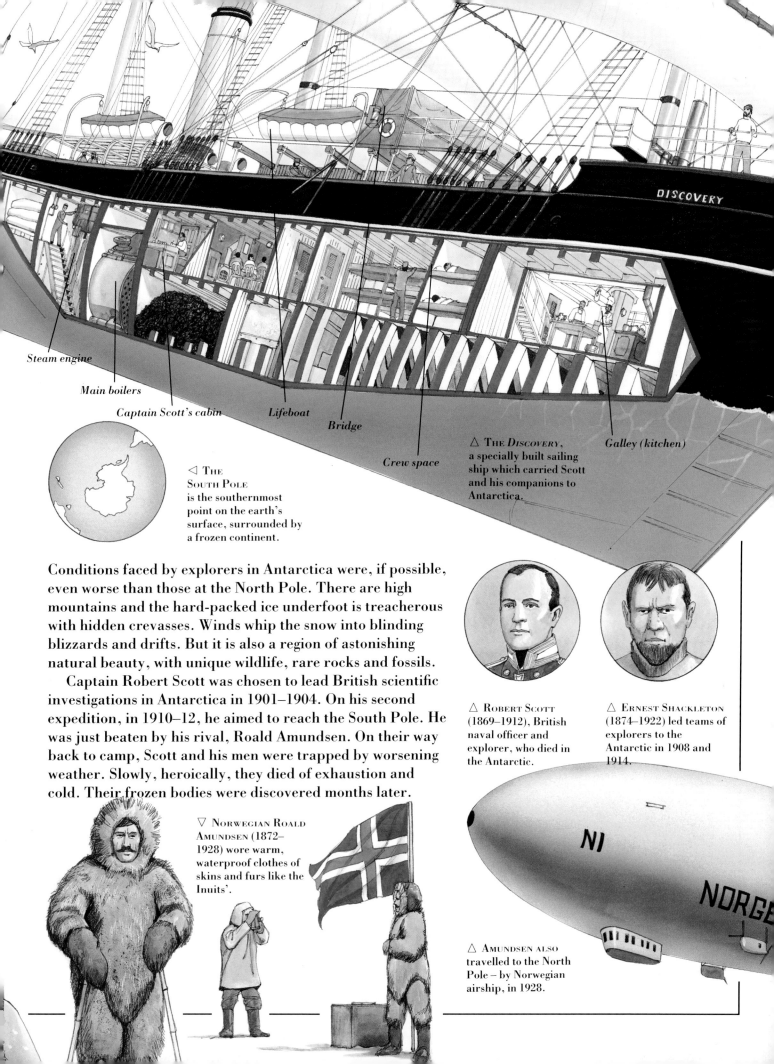

Steam engine

Main boilers

Captain Scott's cabin

Lifeboat

Bridge

Crew space

△ THE *DISCOVERY*, a specially built sailing ship which carried Scott and his companions to Antarctica.

Galley (kitchen)

◁ THE SOUTH POLE is the southernmost point on the earth's surface, surrounded by a frozen continent.

Conditions faced by explorers in Antarctica were, if possible, even worse than those at the North Pole. There are high mountains and the hard-packed ice underfoot is treacherous with hidden crevasses. Winds whip the snow into blinding blizzards and drifts. But it is also a region of astonishing natural beauty, with unique wildlife, rare rocks and fossils.

Captain Robert Scott was chosen to lead British scientific investigations in Antarctica in 1901–1904. On his second expedition, in 1910–12, he aimed to reach the South Pole. He was just beaten by his rival, Roald Amundsen. On their way back to camp, Scott and his men were trapped by worsening weather. Slowly, heroically, they died of exhaustion and cold. Their frozen bodies were discovered months later.

△ ROBERT SCOTT (1869–1912), British naval officer and explorer, who died in the Antarctic.

△ ERNEST SHACKLETON (1874–1922) led teams of explorers to the Antarctic in 1908 and 1914.

▽ NORWEGIAN ROALD AMUNDSEN (1872–1928) wore warm, waterproof clothes of skins and furs like the Inuits'.

△ AMUNDSEN ALSO travelled to the North Pole – by Norwegian airship, in 1928.

TOURISTS

UNTIL THE EIGHTEENTH CENTURY, few people travelled purely for fun. Most travel and exploration – for profit, to win power, to 'do good', to govern, to study, or to make scientific investigations – was a serious business. Unlike today, holidays did not usually involve long journeys. In the past, travel was difficult and dangerous. Not many people would have been prepared to risk life and limb, except for what they felt was a good reason. Religious pilgrims and wandering scholars from many lands and many centuries often enjoyed their travels, but their journeys had a solemn purpose too. And, unlike 'proper' explorers, pilgrims and scholars rarely pioneered new routes, preferring well-trodden ways.

△ FROM ABOUT 1600–1900, rich young men went on a 'Grand Tour' of Europe to study works of art.

◁ TOURISTS HAVE travelled to Eygpt since Greek and Roman times. But the invention of steamships in the 19th century, and the setting up of the first travel agency, run by Thomas Cook, meant that foreign travel became possible for more people. From about 1750, it became fashionable for invalids to go abroad. Doctors advised that warm climates and mountain air would do them good. Anyone unable to walk used a 'bath chair' (*above*), an early wheelchair.

▷ IN THE PAST, travel was often cold and uncomfortable. Coaches, railway carriages and early aircraft had little or no heating. This fur-lined flying costume was designed by Parisian couturier Madeleine Vionnet in 1922.

▽ SHIPS TAKING British families to India sailed through the Strait of Gibraltar.

▽ THE EARLY 20th century was the age of luxurious sea-travel. It could take 6 weeks to sail to South Africa, and 12 weeks to reach Australia. All liners provided good accommodation, fine food and lively entertainment for passengers who went first class.

△ SWIMMING in the sea, from 'bathing machines' like these at Tenby, Wales, first became fashionable in the 18th century. It was thought to be good for health.

Today, in many countries, the tourist trade is a major industry, employing millions of people. How and why has this change taken place? Since the early twentieth century, in many industrialised nations, ordinary working people have been able to claim several weeks' holiday every year as a right. Cheap air fares and well-organised travel agencies have made it easy to travel to places where warm, sunny weather can be guaranteed. Holiday resorts, hotels, camp sites and theme parks all aim to provide accommodation and entertainment to satisfy their visitors. Many people have been taught that taking holidays is good. They hope to feel fitter and work better on their return.

But there is another side to this thriving tourist industry. Economists claim that traditional ways of life – farming, fishing, manufacturing – have been destroyed for ever by mass tourism, especially in poorer lands. And environmentalists warn that unplanned development and uncontrolled pollution are damaging many beautiful and fragile regions of our world.

△ THE FIRST regular passenger flights began c.1920. Planes were small. The largest held 14 passengers, who sat in light wicker chairs, chosen to minimise weight. Passengers were weighed, too. If they were all very heavy, some might be left behind.

▷ FOREIGN HOLIDAYS in sunny resorts first became available to ordinary people in Europe and America in the 1960s. Then, huge 'jumbo jets' made mass travel cheap and easy.

▷ IN THE 1970s and 1980s, special self-contained holiday resorts ('theme parks') became popular.

SPACE

IN 1961, President J. F. Kennedy of the USA declared, 'I believe that this nation should commit itself to achieving the goal, before the decade is out, of landing a man on the Moon…'. In 1969, television viewers worldwide watched in awe as two American astronauts walked on the Moon's surface. Travel in space – the last frontier – was a triumphant reality. Practically and psychologically, the first step on the Moon was, as Moon-walking astronaut Neil Armstrong declared, 'a giant step for mankind'.

△ RUSSIAN cosmonaut Yuri Gagarin (1934–1968), the first man to travel in space.

◁ DESIGN for a spaceship from the Napoleonic period (1800–1815). It is based on hot air balloons, made popular by the Montgolfier brothers, who lived in France in the 18th century.

The 1960s space programme was only possible because of rocket technology developed by German scientists during the 1939–1945 War. Before then, no flying machines could generate enough energy to blast spacecraft through the earth's gravitational field. The Soviet and American governments put huge sums of money into space research; the 'space race' became a matter of political prestige.

The first space flight was in 1957; a Russian unmanned satellite, *Sputnik 1*, orbited the earth. America launched its first satellite later that year. In 1961, Russian Yuri Gagarin became the first person to make a space flight.

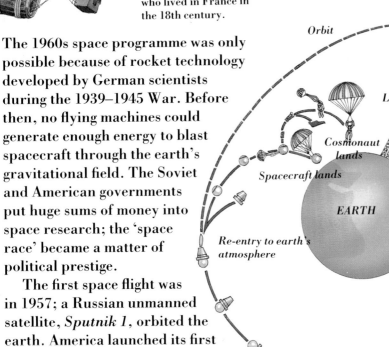

Orbit

Launch

Cosmonaut lands

Spacecraft lands

EARTH

Re-entry to earth's atmosphere

Orbit

Spacecraft

Rocket

△ THE PATH (orbit), one and a half times round the earth, taken by Gagarin's Vostock spacecraft in 1961.

◁ IN JUNE 1965 American astronaut Edward White made the first space walk, tethered by an air-line to his space capsule.

▷ THE ENORMOUS Vostock rocket, over 30 metres high, that blasted Gagarin into space.

Tether/air supply

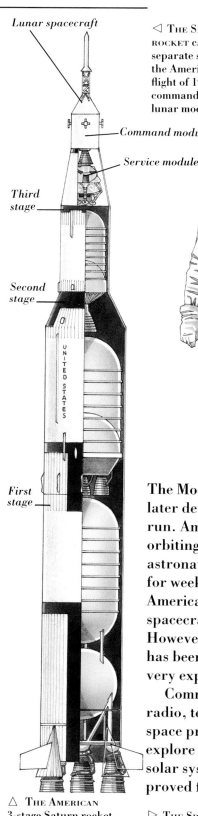

Lunar spacecraft

Command module

Service module

Third stage

Second stage

First stage

◁ THE SATURN ROCKET carried two separate spacecraft for the American moon flight of 1969: a command module and a lunar module.

◁ TRAVELLERS IN SPACE wear special clothing to protect them from extreme temperatures and harmful cosmic radiation.

△ ASTRONAUTS LANDED on the Moon from the lunar module and explored its rocky surface in a battery-powered Lunar Roving Vehicle (*right*). Both machines had to work in conditions of low gravity and extreme temperatures.

The Moon landings were a spectacular technological feat, but later developments may prove more important in the long run. America and the former USSR both built permanently orbiting space stations – huge, well-equipped 'bases' where astronauts can live, work and conduct scientific experiments for weeks at a time. Skylab, the first, was launched by America in 1973. America also designed a reusable spacecraft, the Space Shuttle, launched in 1979. However, although the Shuttle seems a good idea, it has been plagued by problems, and has proved very expensive to operate.

Communications satellites, used to transmit radio, television and telephone signals, and space probes, sent to explore distant parts of the solar system, have proved far more useful.

△ THE AMERICAN 3-stage Saturn rocket, over 60 metres high, which lifted the Apollo moon expedition spacecraft into space. During blast-off, it burned 3 tonnes of fuel (kerosene plus liquid oxygen) per second.

▷ THE SPACE SHUTTLE and its huge booster rockets (with their fuel tank) leaving the launch pad. The Shuttle does not have enough power to escape from the earth's gravity by itself.

Rocket

Reusable shuttle

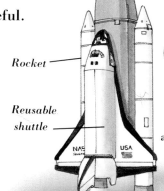

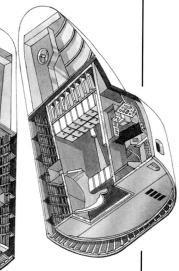

△ INSIDE THE Space Shuttle. Designing the Shuttle was an enormous challenge. In space, it floats like other spacecraft and is steered by small rocket motors. In the earth's atmosphere, it flies like a glider.

PAST AND FUTURE

A TIME TRAVELLER from the 1890s would find the world transformed by many modern inventions. Modern scientific discoveries have also revolutionised our knowledge of the past. Archaeologists now use many different methods to explore the remains of ancient civilisations.

△ IN SCIENTIFIC excavations, the position of each object found is carefully recorded on a grid.

△ DENDRO-CHRONOLOGY, the study of tree-ring growth, helps date wooden objects.

◁ RADIOCARBON DATING is used to discover the age of objects – like wood, bone, shell – that were once alive. All living things soak up Carbon-12 and Carbon-14 from their environment. After death, Carbon-14 decays, but Carbon-12 does not. So the older an object, the less Carbon-14, compared with Carbon-12, remains.

△ ALPHA PARTICLE spectral analysis examines the chemical composition of objects. Different substances combine with minerals in the environment in different ways – giving clues to an object's age.

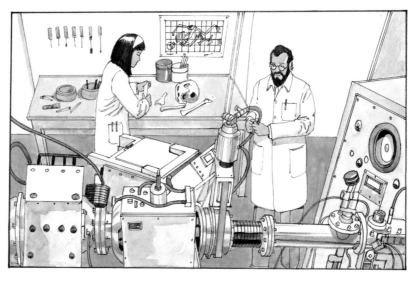

▽ SKILLED CONSERVATORS can preserve ancient manuscripts, like the Dead Sea Scrolls (c. 100 BC), so they may be studied and will not decay.

As well as the techniques shown on this page, archaeologists can take infra-red photographs to see underneath layers of paint on a picture, and photomicrographs to record objects too small to see with the naked eye. X-rays are used to look inside things without disturbing the outer covering. Egyptian mummies are a good example. The bones can be examined without damaging the finely-decorated outer cases. Aerial photos of crop marks can reveal the sites of ancient buildings, and resistivity surveys can show where underground layers of soil have been disturbed in the past. Computers can process data to produce suggestions of what might have happened at a shipwreck, for example, or to draw the missing fragments of a pot. Most of these techniques have one great advantage over old-fashioned excavations: they leave archaeological evidence undamaged for following generations to explore.

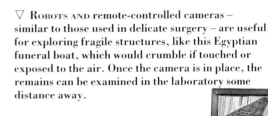

▽ ROBOTS AND remote-controlled cameras – similar to those used in delicate surgery – are useful for exploring fragile structures, like this Egyptian funeral boat, which would crumble if touched or exposed to the air. Once the camera is in place, the remains can be examined in the laboratory some distance away.

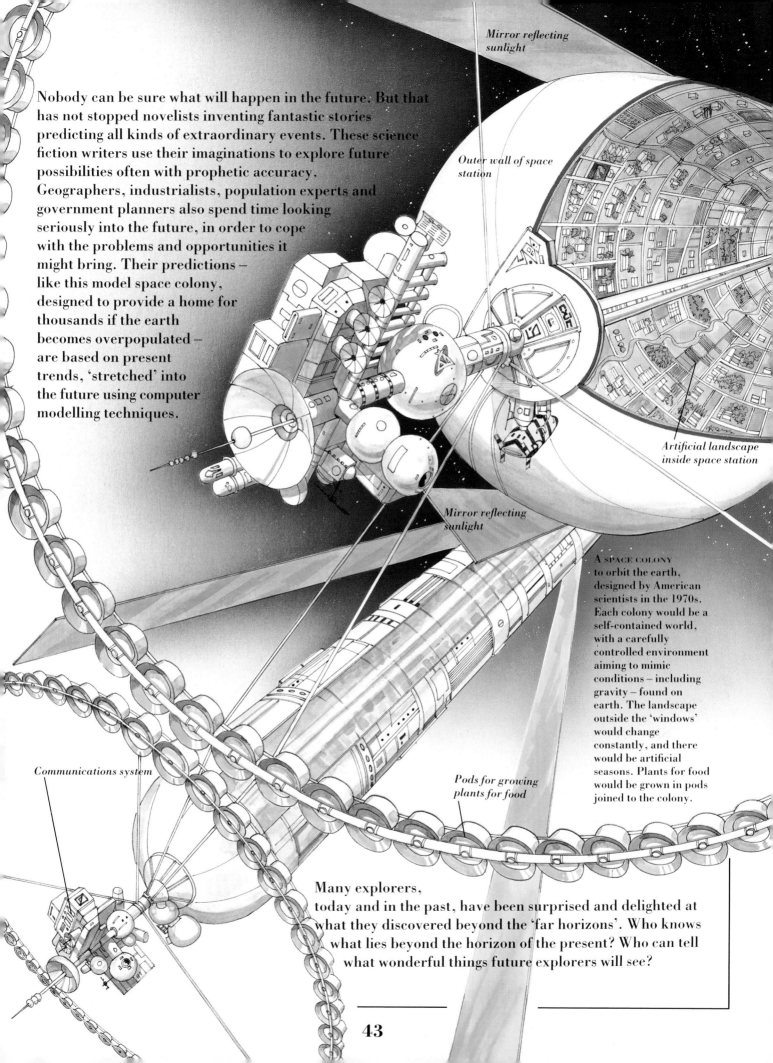

Nobody can be sure what will happen in the future. But that has not stopped novelists inventing fantastic stories predicting all kinds of extraordinary events. These science fiction writers use their imaginations to explore future possibilities often with prophetic accuracy. Geographers, industrialists, population experts and government planners also spend time looking seriously into the future, in order to cope with the problems and opportunities it might bring. Their predictions – like this model space colony, designed to provide a home for thousands if the earth becomes overpopulated – are based on present trends, 'stretched' into the future using computer modelling techniques.

Mirror reflecting sunlight

Outer wall of space station

Artificial landscape inside space station

Mirror reflecting sunlight

A SPACE COLONY to orbit the earth, designed by American scientists in the 1970s. Each colony would be a self-contained world, with a carefully controlled environment aiming to mimic conditions – including gravity – found on earth. The landscape outside the 'windows' would change constantly, and there would be artificial seasons. Plants for food would be grown in pods joined to the colony.

Communications system

Pods for growing plants for food

Many explorers, today and in the past, have been surprised and delighted at what they discovered beyond the 'far horizons'. Who knows what lies beyond the horizon of the present? Who can tell what wonderful things future explorers will see?

43

Early hunter and explorer

TIMELINE

Arab dhows

Phoenician ships in port

BC
1,000,000 Earliest humans begin to spread worldwide from origins in Africa.
40,000 Groups of hunters and gatherers travel south to reach Australia.
30,000 First humans travel across land-bridge to reach North America.
9000 Wandering hunters reach far South America.

Akkadian merchants

5000 Groups of exploring farmers establish first settlements in Mesopotamia.
3000 Inuit explorers travel by sea to Alaska and settle there.
2600 Egyptian sailors make first-recorded voyage, to Lebanon.
2000 Groups of warriors arrive from north to settle in Greece.
2000 First sailors reach Melanesian islands.
1500 Groups of settlers migrate to northern India from eastern Europe.

1493 Egyptian trading expeditions to Punt.
1300 First sailors reach islands of west Polynesia and settle there.
1200 Moses leads Exodus of Jewish people from Egypt to Israel/Palestine.
1100 Phoenician merchants establish trading colonies on distant shores of the Mediterranean.
750 Greek travelling merchants and settlers set up similar colonies.
500 Persian military explorers lead expedition to conquer Central Asia.
c.450 Herodotus travels in Egypt; interviews other Greek travellers and explorers.

Goods traded on the Silk Route

Roman baggage wagon

334–323 Journeys of Alexander the Great of Macedon.

218 Hannibal, commander of army from Carthage, North Africa, leads expedition (with elephants) across the Alps to attack Rome.

c.200–c.AD 200 Roman army commanders and engineers explore and survey lands conquered by Rome.
138 Chinese traveller Chang Chien explores Central Asia.

112 The 'Silk Route' (between China and Europe) first used by travelling merchants.
100 Camels first used by travellers in Sahara Desert. Long journeys now easier.

AD
46–57 Christian missionary journeys in Mediterranean lands made by St Paul. Other missionaries perhaps reach India.
132 Jewish 'diaspora': Jewish people driven from Israel after rebellion against Roman rule; Jews settle in Europe and Asia.
150 Wandering scholars bring Buddhist faith to China from India.
271 Chinese invent magnetic compass.
300 Sailors first reach east Polynesian islands.
449 Groups of Angles, Saxons and Jutes from Europe travel westwards to settle in England.
550 Travelling Korean monks introduce Buddhism to Japan.
622 The Prophet Muhammad and his followers travel from Mecca to find freedom to worship as Muslims elsewhere.
632 The Prophet Muhammad dies; Muslim scholars, officials and soldiers travel to spread the Islamic faith throughout the Middle East.
658 Chinese army commanders now control all Central Asia after years of exploring.
c.800 Viking sailors make first raids in

northern Europe.
860 Vikings reach Iceland.
862 Soldier and explorer Rurik the Viking founds city of Novgorod, Russia.
c.920 Ibn Fadlan explores trade routes in Russia.
986 Vikings colonize Greenland.
c.1000 Leif Eriksson sails to Vinland (America).

Magnetic compass, made around 1500

c.1200 Aztecs arrive in Mexico after years of wandering in the desert.
1206 Mongols (from Mongolia) launch great military expeditions to conquer Central Asia, the Middle East, China and Russia.
1271 Marco Polo begins his travels.
1304 Birth of Ibn Battuta, great Muslim explorer.
1349 Chinese sailors establish settlement at Singapore; Chinese power expands in South-East Asia.
1405 First of Chinese envoy Zheng He's 7 voyages in Indian Ocean.

Indian village

Assyrian barge

44

Crew of Captain Cook's ship Endeavour

Robert Peary, the first man to reach the North Pole

Astronaut in spacesuit

1418 Portuguese sailors begin to explore African coasts and the Atlantic islands (the Canaries, Azores and Madeira).
1487 Bartolomeu Dias sails round Cape of Good Hope.
1492 Columbus sails to America. (Sailors from West Africa may have made the journey before him, but he is the first to return to describe his travels.)

East India Company's coat of arms

1493 First European (Spanish) settlement in America.
1498 Vasco da Gama sails to India.
1501 First African slaves taken to Americas.
1505 Portuguese sailors explore East African coast.

Dr David Livingstone

1509 First watch invented in Nuremberg, Germany. Accurate watches (chronometers) later help sailors calculate their position at sea.
1511 Portuguese sailors reach East Indies.
1519 Spaniard Hernan Cortes begins to explore and conquer Mexico.
1520 Spaniard Magellan sails to the Pacific.
c.1525 First potatoes brought to Europe from America.
1532 Spaniard Pizarro explores and conquers Inca Empire in Peru.
1559 Tobacco first brought to Europe from America.
1581 Russian army commander Yermak explores Siberia.
1596–97 Barents (Dutch) explores Arctic.
1600 British East India Company founded. Dutch Company founded 1602.
1607 First permanent European settlement in North America, at Jamestown.
1615 English sailor William Baffin explores Arctic America.
1620 Pilgrim Fathers reach America.
1645 Abel Tasman (Dutch) makes first voyage round Australia. Sights New Zealand.
1649 First overland crossing of Russia to reach the Pacific.
1681 La Salle explores vast Mississippi basin.
1728 Bering (Denmark) explores Alaska.
1733 Russia sends Great Nordic Expedition to look for sea passage round far

north coast of Asia.
1766—69 French explorer Bougainville sails round the world, making detailed scientific notes and investigations.

The frontier town of Adelaide, Australia

1768 Cook begins first of three voyages to explore the Pacific.
1786 French explorers Paccard and Balmat climb Mont Blanc (highest peak in Europe). Scientific study of mountains begins.
1820 Russian, American and English explorers are first-known people to see continent of Antarctica.
1829 German traveller von Humbolt explores Siberia and nearby lands.
1831–1836 British biologist Charles Darwin makes important discoveries about evolution on voyage to explore Galapagos Islands, in Pacific Ocean.
1838–1842 United States Exploring Expeditions visit Antarctica and North-West Pacific coast.

1850 American Maury makes first attempts to map Atlantic Ocean.
1853 British doctor Livingstone begins explorations in Africa.
1870 Russian explorer Przhevalsky makes important scientific discoveries in Central Asia.
1872 First voyage by *Challenger* to explore oceans.

Yuri Gagarin – the first person to travel in space

1879 Swedish explorer Nordenskiold becomes first person to sail through North-East Passage and right round Asia.
1888 Norwegian explorer Nansen crosses Greenland.
1909 American Peary and his team become first to reach North Pole.
1911 Amundsen (Norway) first to reach South Pole.
1912 English explorer Scott dies in rival South Pole expedition.

1922 Germans are the first to use sonar (sound waves) to explore underwater.
1934 World-record dive by Beebe and Barton.
1953 Explorers Hillary (New Zealand) and Tensing (Nepal) reach summit of Mount Everest – the highest point on earth.
1957 First spaceflight, by Russian Sputnik.
1961 Russian Gagarin is first human to travel in space.
1969 Americans Armstrong and Aldrin are first people to land on the Moon.

The Space Shuttle takes off

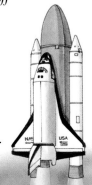

GLOSSARY

Ancestors Earlier generations of our family: grandparents, great-grandparents and so on.

Aqualung Device which allows divers to remain underwater for long periods. Also called scuba: Self-Contained Underwater Breathing Apparatus.

Archaeologists People who study human history through the physical remains of the past.

Archaic Extremely old.

Asia Minor Present-day Turkey and adjoining lands of the Commonwealth of Independent States (formerly USSR).

Astronaut The English and American term for a person trained to travel in spacecraft.

Aztecs The inhabitants of the powerful civilisation which flourished in Mexico, c.1300–1521.

Balm Smooth, sweet-smelling ointment often made from plant oils.

Bathing machine A 'room' on wheels, rather like a caravan. It was pushed (or pulled by a horse) into shallow water, so women could bathe in the sea from it in privacy and safety.

Bathyscaphe Highly specialised submarine to take scientists to the deepest parts of the ocean in a cabin similar to a bathysphere's.

Bathysphere Diving machine, lowered by cable from another ship; globe-shaped and made of thick metal to withstand the pressure of extremely deep water.

Buddhist A follower of the teachings of Indian philosopher Siddhartha Gautama (died 486 BC).

Byzantine Belonging to the civilisation centred on the city of Byzantium (present-day Istanbul, Turkey) which flourished between AD 610–1453.

Central Asia Lands which today form part of China, Iran, Pakistan, Afghanistan and the Commonwealth of Independent States.

Chronometer A very accurate portable clock, used by sailors to calculate longitude, for fixing their position at sea.

Colonial Belonging to a colony.

Colony Settlement established by people of one country, under their own laws, in another land.

Conventional Governed by society's rules; most often used when describing clothes and appearance, formal behaviour, good manners etc.

Cosmonaut The Russian term for someone trained to travel in spacecraft.

Dominant Most powerful.

Draft The depth of a boat in the water (sometimes spelled 'draught').

Dredge To scoop up objects from the seabed, in a bucket, net or shovel.

Envoys High-ranking messengers sent from one government to another.

Evolve To change and become better suited to your surroundings over a long period of time.

Extinct When all members of a particular species of plant or animal have died throughout the whole world.

Gravitational Belonging to gravity, the force that keeps objects (and people) close to the earth.

Ice Age Period when the world becomes colder, and ice covers large areas of land and sea. There have been several ice ages.

Impoverished Having become poor.

Incense Solid perfume, burned during religious ceremonies to create a holy mood.

Indentured Bound by a legal agreement, an indenture, to work as a servant for a number of years.

Islam The faith of Muslim people.

Joint-stock company A business partnership in which a number of people join together to finance a project. They share any profits, according to how much they have contributed at the start.

Kerosene Type of fuel oil burned in jet engines and in spacecraft. It is dangerous because it easily catches fire.

Land-bridge Thin strip of land, with water on both sides, linking two larger areas.

Lateen A triangular-shaped sail, used by coastal shipping in the Mediterranean and Indian Ocean, where winds are usually light. It could not withstand ocean gales.

Latitude Distance north or south of the Equator.

Levant The lands of the Middle East: present-day Lebanon, Syria, Jordan, Israel, Palestine, Egypt.

Longitude Distance east and west, measured since 1884 from the 0° Meridian fixed at the Old Royal Observatory, Greenwich, London.

Mesopotamia The land between the Tigris and Euphrates rivers, where several early civilisations developed. Part of modern Iran and Iraq.

Muslim Someone who worships God following the example of the Prophet Muhammad (died AD 632) and the teachings of the Qur'an.

Myrrh Strong-smelling substance obtained from trees growing in warm countries. Used to make perfumes and, in the past, to preserve dead bodies before burial.

Neanderthal The name of the place in Germany where the remains of an early human creature, now extinct, were first discovered in 1856.

Nomads People who live a wandering life, usually following a seasonal pattern to find grazing for their animals.

Observatory A building, usually equipped with telescopes and other scientific instruments, where astronomers study the stars.

Oracle Somebody, usually a priestess, who is believed to foretell the future.

Orbit Regular path taken by one object around another one. For example, the moon orbits the earth. The earth orbits the sun.

Ottoman The name of a Turkish dynasty of rulers who were powerful from the 15th–19th centuries. Also used to describe the empire they ruled.

Paddle-steamer Ship powered usually by two wheels, fitted with paddles which act like hundreds of oars, pushing the boat through the water. The wheels (one each side of the boat) are turned by steam engines.

Pharaoh The ancient Egyptian kings.

Puritans Religious reformers who lived in England during the late 16th and early 17th centuries. A group of them, known as the 'Pilgrim Fathers', emigrated to America, hoping to live there according to their religious beliefs.

Qur'an The holy book of Muslims, who believe its words were revealed to the Prophet Muhammad by God.

Resistivity survey Archaeological technique that uses electronics to detect past changes in underground soils without disturbing the surface.

Scurvy Disease common to sailors and other long-distance travellers in the past. It was caused by lack of Vitamin C, found in fresh fruit and vegetables.

Soviet Belonging to the former USSR (see USSR). Russia was the most powerful state within the USSR.

USSR (Union of Soviet Socialist Republics) Group of states, formerly ruled as one unit by a Communist government. Since 1991, former USSR territories have ruled themselves. Now known as the Commonwealth of Independent States (CIS).

INDEX

PRINTED IN BELGIUM BY proost INTERNATIONAL BOOK PRODUCTION